BLACK PHOTOGRAPHERS, 1840–1940
An Illustrated Bio-Bibliography

Deborah Willis-Thomas

GARLAND PUBLISHING, INC. • NEW YORK & LONDON
1985

Library of Congress Cataloging in Publication Data

Willis-Thomas, Deborah, 1948–
Black photographers, 1840–1940.

(Garland reference library of the humanities ;
v. 401)
Includes index.
1. Photography—Bio-bibliography.   2. Afro-American
photographers.   I. Title.   II. Series.
TR139.W55   1985   770'.92'2   82-49145
ISBN 0-8240-9147-7 (alk. paper)

Cover design by Laurence Walczak

Printed on acid-free, 250-year-life-paper
Manufactured in the United States of America

ACKNOWLEDGMENTS

Since 1970, photography has been an important part of my life. I would like to express my appreciation for the assistance I have received over the years from my colleagues, family and friends. I am grateful to Anne Tucker, my first instructor in the history of photography at the Philadelphia College of Art, who suggested that I take on this project. I am especially grateful to Dick Newman, who called me asking if I would like to do a book on black photographers, and to James T. deAbajian, for without his entries on photographers in *Blacks in Selected Newspapers, Censuses and Other Sources* many of the names would not have been included. The book's format and organization has benefited from the suggestions of the photographic historian, Gail Buckland.

For permission to reproduce material in their collections, I thank the photographers, collectors and the institutions who so generously made their work available for reproduction, especially John Jezierski and Martha Woodruff.

Finally, I would like to thank Julie Van Haaften, Melvina Lathan, Hank Thomas, Sr./Jr., Luis DePasquale, Diana Lachatanere, C. Daniel Dawson, Anthony Barboza, Frank Stewart, Ernest Kaiser, Jean Blackwell Hutson, Marsha Watts, Steven Jones, Darryl Davis, Edwina Whitlock and my colleagues at the Schomburg Center for Research in Black Culture, International Black Photographers and, most importantly, my family—without their help and support this project would not have been possible.

CONTENTS

FOREWORD

Black Photographers, 1840–1940, An Illustrated Bio-Bibliography, is the product of eleven years of painful, meticulous labor. The author started from scratch and has discovered almost completely forgotten photographers and their works. Her sources were private collections, seldom-used newspaper and magazine files, obscure institutional collections, and the private albums of the relatives of photographers. Her labors have yielded significant results.

This work is a concrete manifestation of a continuous and important activity—documenting the African-American's contributions to the culture of the world. The author has had to address and then disregard the prevailing presumption that in certain fields, such as the visual arts, blacks have not made significant offerings. This belief has become a self-perpetuating state of ignorance, in which researchers and scholars unable to find written evidence have not investigated areas of history they thought unproductive, thereby helping to discourage research in these areas. The existing activities go unrecorded and are thus deemed non-existent. Despite these obstacles, Deborah Willis-Thomas has persisted and has produced an original work of research scholarship.

In addition to its general importance as a source book for the study of photographic history, this book has two other noteworthy features. First, it rescues from obscurity early black photographers and restores them to their rightful place in history by documenting their contributions. For example, who would know that Jules Lion, a black man born in France, was the first photographer to introduce the daguerreotype to New Orleans; or that DeWitt Keith of Washington, D.C., was the "official portrait photographer for the Department of State" whose works were reproduced on U.S. postage stamps? Each made an important contribution to American photographic history and both have been ignored by previous historians.

Because most of these photographers focused their cameras on black subjects, this book serves as a useful new source for finding photographic images of black America. Through the author's efforts, the major chroniclers of black people—black photographers—have been collected and organized in one critical volume. Many know of James Van Der Zee, the prolific recorder of Harlem's history. However, few realize that Ellis L. Weems has done equivalent work in the American south. Working from 1920 until the 1960s, he "amassed a little over 300,000 prints and negatives of the people of Jacksonville" (letter to the author dated July 19, 1974 from the photographer). Now that Mr. Weems' valuable collection has been brought to life, it becomes an excellent tool for clarifying and reconstructing the past.

Deborah Willis-Thomas has produced a much-needed instrument for understanding black America. Moreover, she has underscored one of its contributions to the United States, which is ultimately a donation to the culture of the world. We can all be thankful that this valuable book is now available.

C. Daniel Dawson
Curator of Photography and Film
The Studio Museum in Harlem

INTRODUCTION

The past fifteen years have witnessed a growing interest on the part of historians, collectors, teachers, librarians, artists, and photographers in the history of photography. Old photographs—their subjects and their processes alike—have intrigued many of us during this resurgence. A premier concern of this recent interest has been the attempt to assess the relationship of photography to the fine arts, and a number of books and essays have appeared on the art of photography, the non-art of photography, documentary and social landscape photography, women photographers, Civil War photography, and the collecting of photographic images. With the exception of works by James Van Der Zee and P.H. Polk, none of these books, however, has concerned itself specifically with the black photographers of the nineteenth and early twentieth centuries.

The task of documenting the contributions of black photographers in America has been a difficult one, due in part to the lack of staff time, funds, and expertise of cataloguers and librarians who have filed and catalogued photographs by subject or process and not by photographers. Another obstacle I encountered in my research was the paucity of information available in city directories, newspapers, and periodicals referring to a photographer's activities and/or works. Yet, despite the scarcity of information in these sources, they are among the most important and rewarding guides for documenting the existence and work of black photographers of this period.

Black Photographers, 1840–1940 is not an exhaustive bibliography of black photographers but a working resource of selected photographers born in the United States who were active during the first hundred years of photography. (Additionally, because they worked principally in the United States, French-born Jules Lion and Haitian-born Francis Grice have been included.)

It proved impracticable to include all the black photographers listed in the major city directories; therefore, 65 outstanding figures have been featured. Moreover, hundreds of photographers' works remain unidentifiable or inaccessible in public and private collections. *Black Photographers, 1840–1940* is dedicated to those unknown photographers who charted through their lenses the development of this country and, equally important, the development of black communities. The photographs selected to accompany the entries in this book include every aspect of rural and urban life in America—transportation, politics, social life, military, fraternal organizations, education, families, architecture, and landscapes.

This book is arranged alphabetically by photographers within three chronological divisions reflecting the historical development of different photographic processes.

There are three indexes at the volume's end. Most entries consist of the photographer's name or studio name, birth and/or active dates, geographic location, principal subjects, processes, collections, exhibitions, a selected bibliography, arranged chronologically (books, periodicals, and films) and illustrations of the photographer's works. In the few cases where a photographer's images and/or collections are unavailable, only the name, active dates, geographical location, and sources are cited.

Many of the photographs reproduced here are in public collections and are in fairly good condition. Under the heading "Collections," e.g., Schomburg Center for Research in Black Culture, a researcher may find just one image by one photographer and 20 or more by another. However, with the recent surge of interest by researchers and photograph curators in identifying the works of individual photographers, it seems certain that many more images will come to light.

A case in point—when I began to gather names of black photographers in 1973, there was little active research in this area. I wrote many letters to repositories around the country seeking biographical materials and information about the location of photographs by particular photographers. I was frequently disappointed when my letters were returned with a response written across the bottom. While I recognized this practice as a cost-saving method of answering correspondence, it concerned me that, apparently, these libraries and museums were keeping no records of such requests. Visits to major repositories of black culture proved to be no more fruitful. In 1974 when I visited the Schomburg Center for Research in Black Culture and the Moorland-Spingarn Research Center, neither had created finding aids to photographers represented in their photograph collections. The Library of Congress Photograph Division was one of the few institutions I visited that catalogued photographs by photographer as well as subject and donor. As libraries and historical societies have added photograph curators to their staffs, priority has been placed on identifying photographers and developing appropriate finding aids. Indeed, this shift also occurred at the Schomburg Center, where I have been employed as the Photograph Specialist since 1980.

During the research on this project, I often found a photographer's work scattered across the country. In the case of J.P. Ball, who travelled extensively in the Midwest and the far West, living in Ohio, Minnesota, Montana and Washington, collections of his photographs are to be found throughout these areas. In those cases where collections or individual photographs of a particular photographer are located in different regions, it would appear that the pictures moved around the country with their owners. Hence, the life of the photographs and the photographer has been, for the most part, never the same.

There remains a great need for books, articles, catalogues and exhibitions on black photographers. A few contemporary photographers based in New York have formed a group called the International Black Photographers (IBP) dedicated to acknowledging the contributions of black photographers. To date, they have honored James Van Der Zee, P.H. Polk, Gordon Parks, Moneta Sleet, Jr., Chuck Stewart, Roy DeCarava, Dick Saunders, and Morgan and Marvin Smith. Additionally, as this book goes to press, an exhibition by the Rhode Island School of Design on black photographers, entitled "A Century of Black Photographers 1840–1960" is travelling across the country. Also, a book is being prepared by John Jezierski, Professor of History at

Saginaw Valley State College, entitled *Goodridge Brothers: Saginaw's Pioneer Photographers*, whose life stories are as fascinating as their photographic images.

It is my hope that this bibliography will stimulate and encourage more research in this field and on the black photographer as photojournalist, portraitist, pictorialist, and architectural historian.

Deborah Willis-Thomas
October 1, 1983

GLOSSARY OF PHOTOGRAPHIC PROCESSES: TYPES OF PHOTOGRAPHS MOST COMMONLY FOUND IN PHOTOGRAPH COLLECTIONS

I. *DIRECT POSITIVES*

A. *Daguerreotype* (1839–1855). Invented by a Frenchman, L.J.M. Daguerre, the daguerreotype was the first practical photographic process. A copper sheet, silver plated, was very finely polished and made light sensitive by exposure to iodine vapor in an iodizing box. After exposure in a camera, the latent image was formed by the effect of light and was developed by vapor of mercury heated over a spirit lamp. The mercury attached itself to those parts of the silver iodide affected by light and thus formed a visible image—the mercury appearing very light, the silver dark. The image was "fixed" in a strong salt solution to dissolve away the remaining light-sensitive silver salts. The silver coating of the daguerreotype base gives it a mirror-like surface. The image is visible only from certain angles and tilting the daguerreotype slightly will show a negative image. Sometimes hand-tinted, daguerreotypes were usually fitted into special cases; the most commonly found size today is 2½″ × 3¼″.

B. *Ambrotype* (1852–1870). Also known as a collodion positive, the ambrotype process used a collodion wet plate: prior to exposure, a sheet of glass was coated with nitrocellulose dissolved in ether and alcohol, sensitized with potassium iodide and silver nitrate; this plate was then exposed and developed before the emulsion dried. The glass plates were made in various sizes and placed in decorated cases (often mistaken for daguerreotypes). The glass was backed with black velvet or paper or lacquered in black, causing it to appear positive.

C. *Tintype* (1854–1900). Also called ferrotype or melainotype. Tintypes were introduced in American and used by itinerant photographers who took portraits, especially of Civil War soldiers and landscape views. The tintype was cheap, sturdy, and quick to produce. The emulsion was coated on a sheet of black japanned iron to produce a direct positive image. Many tintypes were mounted in decorated leather cases under glass. As they became more popular, they were placed in card or paper-based matte-like enclosures. They varied in size from 2½″ x 3½″ to ½″ square.

II. *NEGATIVES*

[Paper]

A. *Calotype* (1841–ca.1855). Although rare in America, the calotype was popular in England (where it was patented by William Henry Fox Talbot in 1840) and France. The paper was coated with a solution of silver nitrate, dried, then immersed in a solution of silver iodide. The paper, wet or dry, was then exposed in the camera.

B. *Eastman* (1884–ca.1895). Patented by George Eastman in 1884. The paper was coated with a gelatin base. The resolution quality was very poor.

[Glass]

C. *Collodion* (1851–ca.1880). Glass coated with collodion (pyroxyline dissolved in a mixture of alcohol, ether, bromide, and iodide salts). As soon as the emulsion was set, the plate was immersed in a solution of silver nitrate. This entire procedure had to be done in the dark.

D. *Gelatin Dry Plate* (1878–1920). A sheet of glass was coated with an emulsion consisting of light-sensitive silver halides suspended in a layer of gelatin. Commercially made or ready-made gelatin dry plates were available by 1878.

[Gelatin]

E. *Eastman American Film* (1884–ca.1890). Looks like "film" but is really gelatin. Paper coated with gelatino-bromide emulsion on a substratum of plain gelatin.

F. *Clear plastic (nitro-cellulose)* 1) Extremely thin, curls up and wrinkles easily; roll film. (1889–1903) 2) Non-curl: Somewhat thicker, coated on both sides with gelatin to prevent curling; roll film. (1903–1930) 3) Machine-cut sheet film, rectangular, edges stamped with manufacturer's name. (1913–1939)

G. *Clear plastic (cellulose acetate)* (1939–present). Roll and sheet film, marked "SAFETY" on edge.

III. *PRINTS*

A. *Salt print* or *salted paper print* (ca. 1839–1860). The paper is prepared by soaking it in mild salt water and floating it on a strong solution of silver nitrate to form a coating of silver chloride. The paper was exposed under a negative in sunlight until the image appeared and was then fixed with sodium thiosulphate ("hypo"). Salt prints were often toned in sepia, gold, platinum, or brown colors.

B. *Albumen print* (1850–1895). Introduced by Louis-Desire Blanguart-Evrard in 1850, the albumen print was the standard print used in the nineteenth century. Thin paper was coated with albumen (made from fresh egg whites which were dissolved in potassium iodide and potassium bromide) and then sensitized with a solution of acidified silver nitrate. The paper was exposed to sunlight through a negative until the image appeared. The yellowish paper was toned with sepia colors to enhance the image and prevent fading. The print was later fixed in "hypo" (sodium thiosulphate). Because the paper was so thin, most albumen prints were mounted on board or in albums.

   (1) Carte-de-visite

   Patented in France by Adolphe Eugene Disderi in 1854 and introduced in the United States in 1859, these small prints were mounted on 4¼" x 2½" cards similar in size to a calling card. Most prints were albumen, some were collodion technique. The photographer's name and/or studio were printed on the back of the card. Between 1864 and 1868, American cartes-de-visite were used as a source of Civil War revenues and for the education of slave children. Portraits of emancipated slave children were taken and the photographs sold.

   (2) Cabinet card

   Introduced in the United States in 1866, these 4½" x 6½" cards bore a small print and the photographer's name and address. Most cabinet cards were portraits and so became very popular for stage performers.

C. *Stereograph* (1850–1890). Introduced in the United States in 1859. Stereoscopic photographs were taken either with a camera with two lenses side by side–separated by 2½ inches, the approximate distance between the pupils of human eyes–or with a single-lense camera that took first one picture, then was moved slightly to one side for a second exposure. Most stereographs were made of albumen print and mounted on a 3" x 7" card. The back of the "stereo" lists the photographer's name, address, and type of views available. The stereographs that exist today are mainly records of events and places. However, there are a number of stereoscopic views of blacks in stereotypical roles.

D. *Aristotype* (1818–ca.1910). The light-sensitive part of the emulsion was silver chloride. Gelatin, albumen, or collodion emulsion base was used. This photographic printing paper produces a visible image upon exposure to light without any chemical development. After exposure the print is fixed in sodium thiosulphate ("hypo") and washed.

E. *Platinum print* (1873–1937). Also called platinotype. Patented in England in 1873 by William Willis. The process for making this paper involved sizing the salted paper, then sensitizing it by coating it with a solution containing potassium chloroplatinate and ferric oxalate which was then dried. The image was partly printed out under a contact negative, then further developed in a solution of potassium oxalate, which dissolved the ferrous oxalate and precipitated finely divided metallic platinum, which formed the final image. The print was "fixed" by washing away all remaining iron salts in several successive baths of a weak solution of either hydrochloric acid or citric acid, and then washed. The platinum print used by art photographers had a silver-gray color and was the most beautiful and permanent of the printing papers.

F. *Post card* (1880–present). Introduced in the late nineteenth century, postcards were gravure, halftone, or photographic prints. The photographer was not usually identified.

G. *Silver Print* (1983–present). All modern printing processes are based on this paper. The photographic paper must be chemically treated after exposure to produce a visible image. The discovery of gelatin emulsion changed the technique for making prints as well as negatives. Exposures could be made by artificial light and the latent image developed to a visible one. With the use of gaslight paper (or developing out paper), enlarging became practical. The silver print (also called gelatin-silver) consists of paper coated with gelatin containing light-sensitive silver halides. Printing papers coated with gelatin were introduced in 1882 and had replaced albumen papers by about 1895.

The Photographers

BAILEY, JOHN B.
Active in Boston, Massachusetts, 1840s.

Taught J.P. Ball of Cincinnati the art of
photography.

Rochester Frederick Douglass' Paper, August
31, 1855, p. 1, col. 7 (from *Boston Tele-
graph*). Bailey is listed as a lieutenant
in the Massachusetts Guards.

BALL, JAMES PRESLEY (J.P.)
(1825-?1905) Active in Cincinnati, Ohio;
Helena, Montana; Seattle, Washington.

Ball began photographing in 1845, encouraged
and taught by a black Boston photographer,
John B. Bailey. In that same year, Ball opened
a daguerrean gallery in Cincinnati. The following year, after an unsuccessful year in
Cincinnati, Ball became an itinerant and
travelled to Pittsburgh, Pennsylvania, and
Richmond, Virginia.

Sometime in 1847, Ball was back in Cincinnati
and opened another daguerrean gallery: "Ball's
Daguerrean Gallery of the West." Exhibited in
his gallery was a 600-yard panorama of "Negro
Life in the Ohio, Susquehanna and Mississippi
Rivers." He joined in a partnership with Alexander Thomas, and the name of the business was
changed to Ball and Thomas. Ball travelled
east to learn more about the art of photography,
and upon his return dissolved his partnership,
worked alone for awhile, and then later worked
with his son.

In the early 1870s, J.P. Ball and Son moved
west to Helena, Montana. As opposed to his
portrait photography of whites in Cincinnati,
most of his subjects were of blacks in the
Helena area. He photographed in his studio
as well as on the streets of the developing
West.

Ball is known for his photographs of prominent
people of Cincinnati and Helena.

PRINCIPAL SUBJECTS
Portraits, street scenes, lynchings, funerals,
and crowds.

PROCESS
Daguerreotypes, cartes de visites, cabinet
cards.

COLLECTIONS
James T. de Abajian, private collection, New
York, New York.

Cincinnati Public Library, Cincinnati, Ohio.

Montana Historical Society, Helena, Montana.

Schomburg Center for Research in Black Culture
New York, New York.

SELECTED BIBLIOGRAPHY
Newspapers:

Rochester Frederick Douglass' Paper, April 28,
1854, p. 3, col 6. Also page 2:4. Subscribes
to this paper.

Rochester Frederick Douglass' Paper, May 5,
1854, p. 1 (from *Gleason's Pictorial*). View
and description of his "Great Daguerrean Gallery of the West" (interior view). Mr. Ball

commenced his career as a daguerreotypist in
the year 1845. "Also, there are six of Duncanson's landscapes hanging...." "Mr. Ball
employs 9 men in superintending and executing
the work of the establishment...."

Toronto Provincial Freeman, June 3, 1854, p. 2,
cols. 2-3. News Story from *Gleason's Pictorial*
entitled "Daguerrean Gallery of the West."
Ball commenced his career in 1845.

Cincinnati Daily Enquirer, July 4, 1854, p. 3,
col. 4. "... and we now tell all to whom it
may concern that Ball, No. 28 Fourth Street,
is an artist upon whose abilities all may rely."

Cincinnati Daily Enquirer, July 8, 1854, p. 3,
col. 3. "... by industry, perseverance and
integrity, he has built himself up a business
highly lucrative and respectable. He takes
decidedly the best pictures to be got in Cincinnati."

Cincinnati Daily Enquirer, July 15, 1854. "...
There are 9 artists employed in this gallery,
consequently visitors are not obliged to wait
a whole day for a picture, but can get what
they desire in a few minutes."

Cincinnati Daily Enquirer, July 16, 1854, p. 3,
col. 3. "... Ball takes the best pictures in
this city, has the best operatives in this
country, and the finest gallery in the West.
He has acquired a world wide reputation as an
artist and is well worthy of the praise his
works have received throughout the country...."

Cincinnati Daily Enquirer--advertisement--July
22, 1854.

Toronto Provincial Freeman, June 23, 1855, p.
59, col. 2 (formerly *Herald of Freedom*). Exhibits daguerreotypes at the Ohio Mechanics
Institute Annual exhibition.

Cincinnati Daily Enquirer, September 18, 1856.
Ball had opened a second gallery at 20 West
Fourth Street.

Cincinnati Daily Enquirer, October 25, 1856.
Notice that Mr. Ball was returning from Europe
within a few days.

Cincinnati Daily Enquirer--advertisement--July
22, 1857.

Cincinnati Daily Enquirer--advertisement--July
13, 1859.

Cincinnati Daily Enquirer, July 13, 1859. "...
Mr. Thomas, clerk of Ball's Daguerrean Gallery, has gone East in company with Mr. E.
Ball, brother of the proprietor of the gallery...." "These gentlemen have gone East on
a tour of observation, determined to bring
back with them every improvement in the
Daguerrean art."

St. Paul Western Appeal, March 19, 1887, p. 1,
cols. 3, 4. "He is one of the oldest and best
photographers in the Northwest and is the
only colored man in the business." Advertisement of J.P. Ball, Sr. and Jr. March 26, 1887,
p. 4, col. 3 and April 2, 1887, p. 1, col. 6.

St. Paul Western Appeal, June 18, 1887, p. 4,
col. 2. Attends large picnic (see p. 1) as
photographer.

St. Paul Western Appeal, October 15, 1887, p.
4, col. 1. "... has a lot of the groups
taken on Emancipation Day (including John
Mercer Langston) which he will furnish to
as many as wish them at 5 cents each. He
takes fine cabinets for $1.00 per dozen.

St. Paul Western Appeal, October 28, 1887, p.
1, col. 4. Notice of his removal to Helena
"... before the 1st day of November."

St. Paul Western Appeal, November 19, 1887, p.
4, col. 1. "... we visited his studio ...
and saw several copies of the pictures he
took of the St. James A.M.E. church last
Sunday.... He also has several negatives of
Bishop Brown from which pictures may be had."

St. Paul Western Appeal, December 3, 1887,
p. 4, col. 2. Civil Rights convention dele-
gate.

St. Paul Appeal, May 10, 1890, p. 1, col. 7.
See biography of Robert Harlan (b. 1816) who
in "1848 ... went to California, where, in
a short time, amassed a fortune of $45,000
in gold, which he brought back ... and became the owner of Ball's Photograph Gallery
which he fitted up in a style surpassing any
similar gallery in the country."

Helena Colored Citizen, September 3, 1894,
p. 3, col. 3. "Helena enjoys the notoriety
of having the only colored photographer in
the Northwest.... He is one of the oldest
members now in the profession dating back
to 1845 ... and has had the satisfaction of
taking numerous medals for superior work
over many of the most skillful and artistic
competitors in the largest eastern cities.
Prior to, during, and for several years after
the war, Mr. Ball had one of the largest
and best equipped studios in Cincinnati."

St. Paul Western Appeal, November 23, 1899,
p. 2, col. 6. "J.P. Ball and Son, the re-
knowned photographers, formerly of Minneapolis are here and are doing the best
business in their line in the city."

Seattle Republican, April 20, 1900, p. 4,
col. 1. "Expects father to arrive from Montana and who may permanently reside in
Seattle and operate photography gallery."

Seattle Republican, April 19, 1901, p. 4, col.
1. "Mr. J.P. Ball, Sr. is for the present
doing advertising work on this paper."

Seattle Republican, June 21, 1901, p. 4, col.
2. "Leaves to set up Shriners' lodges in
Portland and plans to then visit Arkansas's
Hot Springs for Rheumatic treatment."

Seattle Republican, January 3, 1902, p. 1,
col. 1. Short account of firm of "Ball &
Sons," photographers.

Books:

Delaney, Martin R. *The Condition, Elevation,
Emigration and Destiny of the Colored People
of the United States.* Philadelphia: privately printed, 1852, p. 118.
    "J. Presley Ball is the principal
    daguerreotypist of Cincinnati, Ohio.
    Mr. Ball commenced the practice of
    his art about seven years ago ... he
    does more business than any in the
    profession in that city. He has a
    brother, Mr. Thomas Ball, and a
    white gentleman to assist him."

Williams, George W. *Negro Race in America*,
Vol. 2. New York: G.P. Putnam's Sons, 1883.

Simmons, William J. *Men of Mark.* Cleveland,
Ohio: G.M. Rewell and Company, 1887, p. 421.

Dabney, Wendell. *Cincinnati's Colored Citizens.*
Cincinnati: The Dabney Publishing Company,
1926, p. 89.

Newhall, Beaumont. *The Daguerreotype in
America.* New York: Duell, Sloan & Pearce,
1961, p. 139.

Rudisill, Richard. *Mirror Image: The Influence
of the Daguerreotype in American Society.*
Albuquerque: University of New Mexico Press,
1971.

de Abajian, James T. *Blacks in Selected Newspapers, Censuses and Other Sources.* Boston:
G.K. Hall, 1974.

BALL, THOMAS
Active in Cincinnati, Ohio, 1850s (see J.P.
Ball).

Woodson, Carter G. "The Negro of Cincinnati
Prior to the Civil War." *Journal of Negro
History*, January 1916, p. 20.

Grimke, Charlotte Forten. *The Journal of Charlotte L. Forten.* New York: Dryden Press,
1953, p. 48. "Mr. Ball is a distinguished
daguerreotypist and artist from Cincinnati.
His elegant establishment is one of the most
profitable and fashionable in the country."

BANNISTER, EDWARD MITCHELL
b. Saint Andrews, New Brunswick (1821-1901).
Active Boston, 1840.

New York City Anglo-American, December 15,
1860, p. 3, cols. 1-2.

U.S. Centennial Commission, International Exhibition, 1876. *Official Catalogue. Part II
Art Gallery ... Sixth and Rev. Ed.* 1876, p.
42.

Simmons, William J. *Men of Mark.* Cleveland, Ohio:
G.M. Rewell and Company, 1887, pp. 816-19.

Negro Year Book 1921-22, p. 294.

Crisis, November 1933, p. 248.

Locke, Alain. *Negro Art: Past and Present.*
Washington, D.C.: Associates in Negro Folk
Education, 1936, p. 16-17.

Negro History Bulletin, October 1941, p. 18.

Negro History Bulletin, April 1949, p. 59.

Porter, James A. *Ten Afro-American Artists.*
Catalog. Washington, D.C.: Washington Gallery
of Art, Howard University, 1967, p. 15.

Perry, Regenia A. *Selections of Nineteenth Century Afro-American Art.* New York: Metropolitan Museum of Art, 1976.

DUNCANSON, ROBERT SCOTT
b. Cincinnati, Ohio (1821-1872).

Rochester Frederick Douglass' Paper, July 22,
1853, p. 2, col. 3 (from *New York Tribune*).
Biographical information.

Rochester Frederick Douglass' Paper, May 15,
1854, p. 1, col. 5 (from *Gleason's Pictorial*).
Mentions his interest in photography.

Toronto Freeman, June 3, 1854, p. 2, cols. 2-
3. A news story (from *Gleason's Pictorial*)
describes J.P. Ball's Daguerrean gallery.
"There are also six of Duncanson's finest
landscapes hanging upon these walls as orna-
ments; among which are the May Party picnic
and the Shepherd Boy—the depth and tone, the
life and beauty of these paintings rank among
the richest productions of American artists."

San Francisco Pacific Appeal, November 14, 1874,
p. 1, cols. 5-6. "Recollections of Charles
Sumner." *Scribners Monthly* article contains
biographical information about Duncanson.

Locke, Alain. *Negro Art: Past and Present*.
Washington, D.C.: Associates in Negro Folk
Education, 1936, pp. 18-20.

Dictionary of Artists in America. 1957.

University of California Los Angeles Art
Galleries, *The Negro in American Art* ...
1967. (Exhibition catalog)

Porter, James A. *Ten Afro-American Artists*.
Catalog. Washington, D.C.: Washington Gallery
of Art, Howard University, 1967, pp. 12-14.

Bearden, Romare, and Henderson, Harry. *Six
Black Masters of American Art*. New York:
Zenith Books, 1972.

Perry, Regenia A. *Selections of Nineteenth
Century Afro-American Art*. New York: Metropolitan Museum of Art, 1976.

GRICE, FRANCIS
b. Port-au-Prince, Haiti.
Active 1855.

Rochester Frederick Douglass' Paper, September 28, 1855, p. 1, col. 1 (from *New York
Tribune*)." Hezekiah Grice ... figures
conspicuously in the erection of steam
engine for these mills ... has a son, a
daguerreotypist and photographist."

Rochester Frederick Douglass' Paper, September 28, 1855, p. 1, col. 1 (from *New York
Tribune*). His daguerrean and wax projects
are described.

San Francisco Elevator, March 30, 1866, p. 2,
col. 4. He moved to San Francisco in 1866.

San Francisco Elevator, August 18, 1867, p. 2,
col. 2. (See biography of father, Hezekiah
(d. 1863).

San Francisco Elevator, April 24, 1868, p. 2,
col. 1. His wax work described. His letter
regarding Haiti, p. 2:4.

San Francisco Elevator, February 5, 1869,
p. 3, col. 3. Advertisement.

Washington New National Era, February 24,
1870, p. 2, col. 6. His letter giving short
description of Elko (Nevada) and a longer
account of Haitian affairs.

San Francisco Elevator, April 8, 1870, p. 3,
col. 4. His letter relating death of John
Freeman and giving excerpts from his mother's
letter from Port-au-Prince.

San Francisco Elevator, April 15, 1870, p. 3,
col. 4. His letter referring to his interests.

HIGGINS, BENJAMIN L.
b. New York, New York; active 1853.

Rochester Frederick Douglass' Paper, February
11, 1853, p. 1, col. 1.

LION, JULES
b. Paris, France (1810-1866).

Originally a lithographer, Lion was active in
photography in the 1840s through the 1860s.

His works concentrated on New Orleans architecture and portraits of its leaders and people.
Through advertisements, Lion generated a public
interest and enthusiasm for the new process--
daguerreotypes.

Lion moved to New Orleans from his native
France in 1837 as a free man of color. He
lived and worked there until his death in
1866 and is credited with introducing the
daguerreotype to New Orleans. By 1840, he
appears to have been fairly well established
in the business of making pictures. The following advertisement describing Lion's work appeared in the *New Orleans Bee* on March 14,
1840:

> DAGUERREOTYPE.--Mr. J. LION, Painter
> and Lithographer, Royal Street. No.
> 10--To comply with the wishes of his
> friends and acquaintances, has the
> honor to announce to the public, that
> on Sunday next, 15th March, at 11
> o'clock precisely, he will give, in
> the Hall of the St. Charles Museum,
> opposite the St. Charles Hotel, a
> public exhibition, in which shall
> be seen the likeness of the most re-
> markable monuments and landscapes
> existing in New Orleans, viz:--the
> Cathedral, Exchange. St. Charles
> Hotel, Royal Street, Town House,
> etc., all made by means of the
> Daguerreotype. Mr. J. Lyon will,
> during the exhibition, make a draw-
> ing which shall be put up at
> lottery.--There shall be as many
> chances as persons present.
>   The price of the lottery tickets
> is $1. Said tickets delivered at
> the entrance.

Also a successful painter, Lion exhibited
at the Exposition of Paris in 1833. He was
awarded an honorable mention for his litho-
graph "Affut aux Canards" (The Duck Blind).
Lion taught art in addition to his other
interests. In 1841, he and M. Canova, another
artist, founded an art school and from 1852
to 1865 he was listed as a professor of drawing at the College of Louisiana.

Unfortunately, there is only one known existing photographic image by Jules Lion. However,
the Louisiana State Museum has documents of
Lion's accomplishments and a number of his
lithographs--among them, the view of St. Louis
Cathedral as it looked in 1840--which is
suspected to be made from a daguerreotype.

PRINCIPAL SUBJECTS
Portraits of New Orleans leaders such as
Jefferson Davis; views of the city's streets
and architecture.

PROCESS
Lithographs, daguerreotypes, tintypes.

COLLECTIONS
Anthony Barboza, private collector, New York,
New York.
The Historic New Orleans Collection, New
Orleans, Louisiana.

SELECTED BIBLIOGRAPHY
Newspapers:

The Courier, March 13, 1840, p. 2, col. 6.

The New Orleans Bee--advertisement--March 14,
1840.

The New Orleans Bee--advertisement--January
5, 1843, p. 4, col. 7.

The New Orleans Bee--advertisement--May 24,
1843, p. 3, col. 4.

New York Times, June 27, 1976, p. 2, col. 30.

New York Times, July 2, 1976, p. 3, col. 21.

Art Journal 36, Fall 1976:48.

National Sculpture Review 25, Fall 1976:3.

Connoisseur 193, November 1976:48.

The Crisis 83, November 1976:316.

American Art Review 3, November/December 1976:
   108; 109, 110.

Apollo 104, December 1976:110.

Contemporary Art/Southeast 1, April/May 1977:
   42.

Louisiana History, Vol. XX, No. 4, Fall 1979, pp.
   397-99. Account of Lion's work as a New
   Orleans photographer.

Books:

Groce, George C. *The New-York Historical Society's Dictionary of Artists in America*. New
   York: New-York Historical Society, 1957.

Newhall, Beaumont. *The Daguerreotype in America*.
   New York: Duell, Sloan & Pearce, 1961.

Rinhart, Floyd, and Rinhart, Marion. *American
   Daguerrean Art*. New York: Potter, 1967, p.
   124.

Wiesendanger, Martin, and Wiesendanger, Margaret. *Nineteenth Century Louisiana Painters
   from the Collection of W.E. Grove*. Gretona,
   Louisiana: Pelican, 1971, p. 67.

Driskell, David. *Two Centuries of Afro-American
   Art*. Catalog. 1976, pp. 36-38, 50, 121.

Perry, Regenia. *Selections of Nineteenth Century
   Afro-American Art*. Catalog. New York: The
   Metropolitan Museum of Art, 1976.

O'Neill, Charles Edwards, S.J. "Fine Arts and
   Literature; 19th Century Louisiana Black
   Artists and Authors." In *Louisiana's Black
   Heritage*, Robert R. MacDonald, John R. Kemp,
   and Edward F. Haas, eds. New Orleans:
   Louisiana State Museum, 1979, pp. 63-84.

REASON, CHARLES L.
(1818-1893); active New York.

Rochester Frederick Douglass' Paper, November
   9, 1855, p. 3, col. 3. Letter of Isaiah C.
   Weaver: "He has volunteered to be my daguerreotypist, and to give to the public, pictures gratis."

Simmons, William J. *Men of Mark*. Cleveland,
   Ohio: G.M. Rewell and Company, 1887, pp. 798-
   804.

RUTTER, THOMAS
(Civil War photographer)

Cobb, Josephine. "Photographs of the Civil
   War." *Military Affairs*, Vol. XXVI, No. 3,
   Fall 1962, p. 131.

WASHINGTON, AUGUSTUS
(1820-?)

Washington's father (an ex-slave) and Asian
mother lived in Trenton, New Jersey, where he
was born. He was well educated and, by the time
he reached his teenage years, had been influ-
enced by his readings of anti-slavery publica-
tions and by the abolitionists meetings he
attended. These political interests were re-
flected in his photography--he took portraits
of many abolitionists, such as William Lloyd
Garrison, in the New England area. In addition, he was an activist for the abolishment
of slavery and the education of blacks.

After a brief career as a teacher in Brooklyn,
New York, Washington moved to Hartford, Connec-
ticut, in 1843 and opened a daguerrean studio
to help finance his college education at the
Kimball Union Academy and later at Dartmouth
College in Hanover, New Hampshire.

Washington advertised his Daguerrean studio
in one of Connecticut's anti-slavery newspapers as well as in other Hartford papers,
stating that his studio was the oldest Daguerrean establishment in the city and that he
employed some of the best artists in the country. In 1847 he opened another Daguerrean
studio in Hartford, but left it the following
year to travel. However, by 1850 he was once
again operating the studio. His galleries
appeared to be very successful in Hartford as
well as in New Hampshire. In early 1854,
Washington immigrated to the African colony
of Liberia, believing that only Africa could
be the black man's home in this world. In
Liberia, he worked as a school teacher, a
daguerreotypist, farmer, and store proprietor.

PRINCIPAL SUBJECTS
Portraits.

PROCESS
Daguerreotypes.

COLLECTIONS
The Connecticut Historical Society, Hartford,
Connecticut.

Schomburg Center for Research in Black Culture,
New York, New York.

SELECTED BIBLIOGRAPHY

New York City Ram's Horn, November 5, 1847,
   p. 4, col. 5. Advertisement. "Washington
   is now executing most beautiful and correct
   miniatures of the New York plan from $1.50
   to $10.00 according to the size and style of
   the plates, cases, frames or lockets."

Rochester North Star, April 7, 1848, p. 2,
   col. 6.

Broadside advertising "The Washington Daguerrean Gallery, Hartford," July 20, 1851.

Hartford Daily Courant--advertisement for the
   Washington Daguerrean Gallery--October 8,
   1952, p. 3, col. 1.

Delaney, Martin R. *The Condition, Elevation,
   Emigration and Destiny of the Colored People
   of the United States*. Philadelphia, 1852,
   p. 126.
   Excerpt:
      "Augustus Washington, an artist of
      fine taste and perception, is num-
      bered among the most successful
      Daguerreotypists in Hartford. His
      establishment ... is perhaps the
      only one in the country that keeps
      a female attendant and dressing
      room for ladies. He recommends, in
      his cards, black dresses to be worn
      for sitting and those who go un-
      suitably dressed are supplied with
      drapery and properly enrobed."

Rochester Frederick Douglass' Paper, November
   25, 1853, p. 4, col. 4 (from *New York Journal*

of Commerce). Sails from New York City on
the Isla de Cuba for Liberia, "well educated,
and quite a gentlemen [sic]."

Rochester Frederick Douglass' Paper, May 11,
1855, p. 2, col. 5 (from *New York Tribune*).
The President of Liberia, Joseph J. Roberts,
takes exception to Washington's letter printed
in the *New York Tribune*.

Rochester Frederick Douglass' Paper, May 18,
1855, p. 2, col. 3 (from *New York Tribune*).
Letter by George T. Downing supports Washington; editorial comment by Douglass.

Rochester Frederick Douglass' Paper, May 18,
1855, p. 2, col. 6. "... a successful mer-
chant, he having discontinued his daguerreotype business, when his first stock of
material was exhausted as he could do better
in other ways, although he received upwards
of $1,000 for daguerreotypes the first years
of his residence there. He has now a fine
sugar farm on the St. Paul's river...."

Anglo American, September 3, 1859, p. 3, col.
4. Washington's activities in Liberia.

Journal of Negro History, April 1925, pp.
286-97 Washington's long letter about his
life and activities as a photographer.

"Augustus Washington, Black Daguerreotypist
of Hartford." *The Connecticut Historical
Society Bulletin*, Vol. 39, No. 1, January
1974.

Connecticut Historical Society's Bulletin,
April 1974.

de Abajian, James T. *Blacks in Selected Newspapers, Censuses and other Sources*. Boston:
G.K. Hall, 1974.

ASHER, ELDRIDGE
Active in Hartford, Connecticut, 1866.

Hartford Daily Courant, p. 301. Advertisement.

BAKER, HATTIE
Active in Cleveland, Ohio, 1887.

Cleveland Gazette, January 15, 1887, p. 4,
  cols. 1, 2. Baker's advertisement as a
  photograph enlarger.

BARNES, J.F.
Active in Syracuse, New York, 1880s.

Cleveland Gazette, March 14, 1885, p. 1, col.
  6. Advertisement for opening of Barnes'
  studio.

BEASLEY, D.E.
Active in St. Paul, Minnesota, 1890s.

St. Paul Appeal, September 19, 1891, p. 3,
  col. 1. "[Beasley] ... is the real proprietor
  of the photograph gallery, corner of Seventh
  and Minnesota Streets."

BOWDRE, HAYES LOUIS
Active in Springfield, Ohio, 1860s-1880s.

Cleveland Gazette, December 29, 1884, p. 1,
  col. 2. Obituary.

BOYD, WALTER A.
Active in New York, New York, 1880s.

Cleveland Gazette, July 9, 1887, p. 1, col. 1.
  "[Boyd] ... has been recently appointed
  general superintendent of the large photograph establishment of D'Anna and Co. He is
  the only colored artist in the establishment."

BRYANT, HAYWARD
Active in Little Rock, Arkansas, 1890s.

St. Paul Appeal, October 31, 1891, p. 1, col.
  5.

St. Paul Appeal, November 21, 1891, p. 1,
  col. 5. Listed as "Little Rock's Colored
  artist and photographer."

DAVIS, C.J.
Active in Philadelphia, Pennsylvania, 1880s.

Photographs including cabinet cards and cartes
  de visites are in the private collection of
  Betty Lawrence, Philadelphia, Pennsylvania.

St. Paul Western Appeal, July 28, 1886, p. 1,
  col. 6. Davis attended a meeting of the
  National Photographers Association in
  Minneapolis.

FARLEY, JAMES CONWAY
(1854-?1910)

The son of slaves, Farley was apprenticed at

an early age to a baker but quit in 1872 to
work as a phototechnician in a photographic
chemical department in Richmond, Virginia.
By 1875, he worked as an operator (the person
who actually sets the scene and takes the picture) with one of Richmond's largest studios--
G.W. Davis Photographic Gallery. The Gallery
employed 5 operators, including Farley, as
well as darkroom technicians. The four white
operators objected to the employment of Farley
and demanded that he be fired; instead, *they*
were fired and Farley became sole operator
for the busy gallery.

Farley exhibited his photographs at the 1884
"Colored Industrial Fair" in Richmond and at
the 1885 "World Exposition" in New Orleans.
In 1895, he opened his own studio, the Jefferson Fine Art Gallery. Farley specialized in
photographing individuals and groups, then
printing them onto playing cards. He took
the portraits of leading society members and
businessmen in the Richmond area.

PRINCIPAL SUBJECTS
Portraits.

PROCESS
Cabinet cards.

COLLECTIONS
Valentine Museum, Richmond, Virginia.

Virginia Historical Society, Richmond, Virginia.

SELECTED BIBLIOGRAPHY

Richmond Planet, February 21, 1885, p. 1,
  col. 3.

Simmons, William J. *Men of Mark*. Cleveland,
  Ohio: G.M. Rewell and Company, 1887, pp. 801-
  804; New York: Arno Press, 1968 (reprint).

Richmond City Directory. 1895-1910

Richmond Planet, May 11, 1895, p. 1.

Richmond Planet, August 31, 1895, p. 4, col. 3.

Richmond Planet, September 7, 1895, p. 4, col.
  1. Describes interior of gallery.

Richmond Planet, June 27, 1896, p. 1.

Richings, C.F. *Evidences of Progress Among
  Colored People*. Philadelphia: G.S. Ferguson,
  1905, pp. 495-496.

Jet Magazine, August 8, 1974, p. 8.

FIELDS, GEORGE
Active in Toledo, Ohio, 1880s.

Cleveland Gazette, December 13, 1884, p. 2,
  col. 5. Biography of Fields.

Cleveland Gazette, January 31, 1885, p. 2,
  col. 3. Gallery mentioned.

Cleveland Gazette, July 25, 1885, p. 2, col.
  3 and p. 4, col. 2. Gallery destroyed by
  fire; loss of $2500.

Cleveland Gazette: May 15, 1886, p. 4, col. 1.

FREEMAN, DANIEL
b. Alexandria, Virginia (1868-?).
Active Washington, D.C., early 1900s.

Freeman studied photography at an early age
with the well-known Washington photographer
E.J. Pullman. He also studied painting and
drawing in Washington's public schools and,
combining these interests throughout his career,

often painted the scenery sets in his studio and designed hand-crafted frames. Freeman opened his first studio in Washington in 1885, claiming to be the first black photographer in that city. Advertisements state that "his gallery is fitted up with all the latest and most approved apparatus; his instruments alone costing over $500." In 1895, Freeman installed the exhibit of the District of Columbia in the Negro Building at the Atlanta Exposition.

PRINCIPAL SUBJECTS
Portraits.

PROCESS
Cabinet cards, silver prints.

COLLECTIONS
Schomburg Center for Research in Black Culture, New York, New York.

SELECTED BIBLIOGRAPHY

Hilyer, Andrew F. *The Twentieth Century Union League Directory: A Historical, Biographical and Statistical Study of Colored Washington, at the Dawn of the Twentieth Century and after a Generation of Freedom.* Washington, D.C., January 1901. Privately printed.

GOODRIDGE BROTHERS
Active in York, Pennsylvania, 1850s; active in East Saginaw, Michigan, 1860s-1880s.

Successful photographers and ambrotypists, Glenalvin, Wallace, and William Goodridge began their careers in York, Pennsylvania, in the 1850s. Shortly before the family was forced to move out of York in 1863 (because of their father's activities with the Underground Railroad), Glenalvin won the prize for "best ambrotypes" at the York County Fair. The Goodridge brothers settled in East Saginaw, Michigan, in 1866, and by 1867 had opened their first studio at 104 N. Washington Street. There are no records indicating Glenalvin's activities in East Saginaw after 1867. Sometime in 1872 Wallace and William built another studio at 220-222 S. Washington Street because fire destroyed the studio at 104 N. Washington. The brothers advertised their capability of taking photographs at night using flash photography. In 1884 they were commissioned by the Department of Forestry to photograph views of the Saginaw Valley. The Goodridge brothers are noted for their portraits of the citizens of Saginaw and pictorial views of the Saginaw Valley.

PRINCIPAL SUBJECTS
Portraits, landscapes of Saginaw Valley and lumberyards.

PROCESS
Cartes de visites, cabinet cards, stereographs.

COLLECTIONS
Public:

Clarke Historical Library, Central Michigan University, Mt. Pleasant, Michigan.

Hoyt Library, Saginaw, Michigan.

New York Public Library, Photography Division, New York, New York.

Saginaw County Historical Society Museum, Saginaw, Michigan.

The Saginaw News, Saginaw, Michigan.

Private:

Anthony Barboza, New York.

Douglas Dougherty, Michigan.

Margaret Griffin, Michigan.

John V. Jezierski, Michigan.

William Oberschmidt, Michigan.

David Tinden, Michigan.

Thomas Trombley, Michigan.

SELECTED BIBLIOGRAPHY

The Goodridge Brothers: Saginaw's Pioneer Photographers. The Saginaw Art Museum, January 10-February 28, 1982. Exhibition catalog.

Cleveland Gazette, March 2, 1889, p. 1, col. 2. "The Goodridge Bros. recently received an order for 14 views from the Agricultural Dept. at Washington, the order coming from the Chief of Forestry division. They will be placed on exhibition at the Parks Exposition this year."

Cleveland Gazette, August 20, 1887, p. 1, col. 1. Describes activities of the firm.

Cleveland Gazette, February 18, 1881, p. 1, col. 2. "[The Goodridge brothers] ... are successfully taking pictures at midnight by the flash process."

New York City Anglo African, August 2, 1859, p. 2, col. 6. Discusses work by Glenalvin Goodridge.

Cleveland Gazette, April 14, 1886, p. 1, col. 1a. Describes William Goodridge taking landscape views for his "Illustrated Michigan."

Rochester Frederick Douglass' Paper, August 26, 1853, p. 3, col. 5 (formerly *Voice of the Fugitive*). Wallace Goodridge visits Canada.

Cleveland Gazette, August 20, 1887, p. 1, col. 1. Describes activities of the firm.

GRAY, J.H.
Active in Minneapolis, Minnesota, 1859; Saginaw Valley, Michigan, 1877.

Cleveland Gazette, July 2, 1887, p. 2, col. 5. Biography and portrait. Gray worked as an assistant in the Goodridge studios.

HUNSTER, LEWIS P.
Active in Springfield, Ohio, 1880s.

Cleveland Gazette, April 17, 1886, p. 1, col. 6. Photographs by Hunster of the Fisk Jubilee Singers.

Cleveland Gazette, April 24, 1886, p. 1, col. 7. "... never before has Mr. L.P. Hunster convinced the public of his ability as an artist, as in the portrayal of the character pictures of Mr. Ed Coates, our far-famed comedian and Mr. Hayes Bowdry, who does tragic and pathetic work in an electrifying style."

Cleveland Gazette, May 16, 1886, p. 1, col. 4. Hunster elected secretary of the Photographers' Union, organized the previous week.

Cleveland Gazette, May 14, 1887, p. 2, col. 7.

Cleveland Gazette, November 5, 1887, p. 1, col. 3.

HUSBAND, HARVEY
Active in Louisville, Kentucky, 1880s.

Cleveland Gazette, November 28, 1885, p. 1,
col. 1. "... one of the leading photographers
is a young colored man."

JACKSON, ANDREW F.
Active in Dayton, Ohio, 1880s.

Cleveland Gazette, September 4, 1886, p. 3,
col. 2.

JOHNSON, JOHN W.
Active in Wilkesbarre, Pennsylvania, 1880s.

Cleveland Gazette, March 5, 1887, p. 1, col.
6. "[Johnson] ... has returned from his
visit to the 'Smoky City,' and is studying
photography."

LAWSON, W.H.
Active in Louisville, Kentucky, 1880s.

St. Paul Western Appeal, August 20, 1887, p.
1, col. 4. "[Lawson] ... is a first class
artist and does a large business painting
banners and preparing regalias for societies."

St. Paul Western Appeal, March 23, 1889, p.
1, col. 2. "Preparing the opening of a
photograph gallery on Walnut Street between
Ninth and Tenth."

LEE, EDWARD HENRY
Active in Chicago, Illinois, 1880s-1890s.

Chicago Conservator, September 8, 1883, p. 4,
col. 4.

St. Paul Appeal, January 10, 1891, p. 2, col.
1. Describes his relationship with the newspaper as an illustrator.

St. Paul Appeal, January 10, 1891, p. 3, col.
4. "[Lee] ... is now thoroughly equipped
for taking cabinet photographs at the residence of his patrons.... He is the first to
attempt photographing without a skylight...."

St. Paul Appeal, May 9, 1891, p. 4, cols. 3-4.

St. Paul Appeal, June 27, 1891, p. 2, col. 3.
Describes his portraits of African Methodist
Episcopal bishops.

St. Paul Appeal, December 19, 1891, p. 2, col.
2. Lists prices of his portraits.

LYNCH, JOHN ROY
b. Louisiana (1847-1939).

Born into slavery in 1847, Lynch remained
enslaved until The Emancipation Proclamation.
He later attended night school, worked as a
photographer's assistant, later as a photographer and at the age of 24 became speaker of
the Mississippi House of Representatives (1873).

Cleveland Gazette, June 14, 1884, p. 1, col.
3. "While still a very young man he started
in business for himself as a photographer."

Cleveland Gazette, October 3, 1885, p. 1.
Biography and portrait.

Simmons, William J. *Men of Mark*. Cleveland,
Ohio: G.M. Rewell and Company, 1887, pp.
748-51.

Lynch, John Roy. "In the Photography Business."
Reminiscences of an Active Life. John Hope
Franklin, ed. Chicago: University of Chicago
Press, 1970, pp. 39-43.

MILLER, J.W.
Active in Mexico, Missouri, 1880s.

Cleveland Gazette, June 8, 1889, p. 1, col. 1.
"[Miller] ... is the only colored photographer in Missouri."

MINTER, C.W.
Active in Kansas City, Kansas, 1880s.

Topeka American Citizen, February 1, 1887,
p. 4, cols. 1-2.

MYZELL, THESTUS
Active in San Francisco, California, 1880s.

Listed in *San Francisco City Directory*.

PERRYMAN, F.R.
Active in Chicago, Illinois, 1880s.

Perryman was an engraver as well as photographer.

Cleveland Gazette, April 6, 1889, p. 3. "...
This is the only colored copying house in
the world."

ROSS, W.H.
Active in Sacramento, California, 1870s.

Listed in *Sacramento City Directory*.

SHEPHERD, HARRY (HENRY)
Active in St. Paul, Minnesota, 1880s.

Shepherd opened his first portrait gallery
in 1887, where he employed 8 attendants. His
first year in business was a very successful
one, with profits amounting to $7,587.50.
Shepherd advertised that "his patrons are
among all classes--from the millionaires to
the day wage worker." The following year,
Shepherd opened two additional studios: the
People's Gallery and the Annex. Shepherd
boasts "the Annex studio is prepared to take
tintypes by electric light at night, this is
a novel feature in the business and is doing
well." A popular photographer, Shepherd ex-
perienced price wars with his competitors:
his competitors sold photographs cheaper
than the $3-$5 that Shepherd charged for his
cabinets, and yet his business did not suffer.
In 1889 his end-of-year profit was $9,000.

Shepherd won first prize (a gold medal) at
the 1891 Minnesota State Fair, and he exhibited
photographs of the Tuskegee Institute at the
Paris Exposition in 1900. Shepherd was one of
the few black members of the National Photographers Association of America at the turn of
the century.

PRINCIPAL SUBJECTS
Portraits and scenes of Tuskegee Institute.

PROCESS
Albumen prints, cabinets, cartes de visites, and tintypes.

COLLECTIONS
Library of Congress, Washington, D.C.
Minnesota Historical Society, St. Paul, Minnesota.

SELECTED BIBLIOGRAPHY

St. Paul Western Appeal, July 28, 1888, p. 1, col. 6. Shepherd attends a meeting of the National Photographers Association.

St. Paul Western Appeal, July 13, 1889, p. 2, cols. 2-3. Describes at length Shepherd's purchase and successful operation of the Peoples' Gallery and McFadden & Co.

St. Paul Appeal, September 28, 1889, p. 1, col. 1. Short description of his tintype process.

St. Paul Appeal, July 12, 1890, p. 3, col. 2. News story.

St. Paul Appeal, September 26, 1891, p. 3, col. 1. Shepherd wins gold medal at the Minnesota State Fair.

St. Paul Appeal, February 7, 1891, p. 3, col. 2. He moves because of fire.

St. Paul Appeal, December 19, 1891, p. 3. Advertisement listing the photograph companies founded by him.

Seattle Republican, March 6, 1900, p. 1, col. 4. Shepherd is discharged from the Paris Exposition for "revolutionary utterances."

Taylor, David Vassar. *Blacks in Minnesota: A Preliminary Guide to Historic Sources.* St. Paul: Minnesota Historical Society, 1976.

THOMPSON, FANNIE J.
Active in Memphis, Tennessee, 1880s.

Cleveland Gazette, January 17, 1885, p. 4, col. 1.

Cleveland Gazette, February 20, 1886, p. 4, col. 3.

Cleveland Gazette, May 22, 1886, p. 1, col. 1. "[Thompson] ... will devote her school vacation to the study of photography."

BATTEY, CORNELIUS M.
(1873-1927)

Born in Augusta, Georgia, Battey lived most
of his life in the north and by 1900 had
established his reputation as a photographer
in the portrait studios in Cleveland and New
York City. He was known there for his portraits
of musicians and members of the Masonic temple.

In 1916 Battey moved from New York to Tuskegee,
Alabama, and shortly thereafter became head
of the Photograph Division of Tuskegee Institute. In addition to photographing local
scenes and people, he made portraits of Paul
Laurence Dunbar, Frederick Douglass, W.E.B.
DuBois, Booker T. Washington, Robert Moton,
and Calvin Coolidge. Battey exhibited his work
and won awards in both American and European
galleries.

An editorial described Battey's life "as one
increasing struggle to liberate, through a
rigid medium, the fluid graces of an artist's
soul. For paint brush and palette, he used a
lens and shutter." (*Opportunity*, May 1927,
p. 126.)

PRINCIPAL SUBJECTS
Portraits of famous black leaders and entertainers, pictorial photographs, photojournalist studies of Tuskegee Institute.

PROCESS
Platinum prints, silver prints.

COLLECTIONS
Larry Gross, New York, New York (private
collector).

Library of Congress, Washington, D.C.

Schomburg Center for Research in Black Culture,
New York, New York.

Tuskegee Institute, Tuskegee, Alabama.

SELECTED BIBLIOGRAPHY

Crisis, November 1915. Cover photograph.

Crisis, May 1917, p. 32. Battey recognized
in Men of the Month; includes photograph.
"Mr. C.M. Battey is one of the few colored
photographers who has gained real artistic
success."

Crisis, September 1918, p. 13. A series of
portraits of "Our Master Minds" has been
issued by C.M. Battey of the Photograph
Division of Tuskegee Institute. It includes
photographs of Frederick Douglass, Booker
T. Washington, John Mercer Langston, Blanche
Bruce, and Paul Dunbar.

Crisis, September 1918, p. 239.

Crisis, April 1919, p. 272. Photograph of
W.E.B. Dubois.

Crisis, November 1919. Cover photograph.

Crisis, December 1919. Cover photograph.

Crisis, March 1920. Cover photograph.

Crisis, April 1920. Cover photograph.

Brownies' Book, April, 1920, p. 109. "...
I shall send you some special child studies
to use. [in *The Brownies' Book*]." Letter
from C.M. Battey.

Crisis, October 1921, p. 274. Mention in "The
Horizon."

Freeman 4, January 25, 1922:472.

Crisis, June 1923, p. 73. Mention in "The
Horizon."

Opportunity, September 1923, p. 279.

Crisis, September 1923. Cover photograph.

Crisis, October 1923, p. 149.

The Tuskegee Messenger, March 11, 1927.
Obituary.

Opportunity, May 1927, p. 126.

Crisis, May 1927, p. 91. Obituary.

Crisis, June 1927, p. 268.

Crisis, October 1927, p. 268. Mention in
"Along the Color Line" (includes photography).

Opportunity, December 1928, p. 369.

Note from E.B. Smith to Harry A. Williamson,
ca. 1930s. Smith was a Masonic leader in
Tuskegee, Alabama, and was Pal's second
husband. "This is my Pal in a characteristic
pose. The picture was taken by her former
husband, Mr. C.M. Battey, who was trained
with Underwood and Underwood of New York
City. They are international photographers.
Mr. Battey was a wonderful photographer;
his passing was a serious loss to our Race."

Ellis, Ethel M., compiler. *Opportunity:
Journal of Negro Life.* Cumulative Index
Volumes 1-27, 1923-1949. New York: Kraus
Reprint Co., 1971, p. 117 (Poem by and
photograph of Battey).

BEDOU, ARTHUR P.
(1882-1966)

Bedou was born in New Orleans and was listed
in the *New Orleans City Directory* as a photographer for over 50 years. In 1922, he also
became co-founder of the People's Life Insurance Company of Louisiana. Recognized as
an artist and journalist, Bedou won awards
for his work and was published in numerous
periodicals. He is best known for his portraits documenting the public and private life
of Booker T. Washington (who was then president of Tuskegee Institute, Alabama). In
addition, Bedou photographed local rallies,
celebrations, individual and school children
portraits, and the Mississippi and Louisiana
countrysides. The luminance of his landscape
photography is particularly admired today.

PRINCIPAL SUBJECTS
Portraits, events, and pictorial scenes of
Mississippi and Louisiana.

PROCESS
Silver prints.

COLLECTIONS
Amistad Research Center, New Orleans,
Louisiana.

Library of Congress, Washington, D.C.

Schomburg Center for Research in Black
Culture, New York, New York.

Tuskegee Institute, Tuskegee, Alabama.

SELECTED BIBLIOGRAPHY

Historic New Orleans Collection, *City Directory of New Orleans 1900-1966.*

*Gulfside Association: Pictures of Scenes and
Activities.* Journal of the Eighth Annual
Meeting of the New Orleans Area Council,
Methodist Episcopal Church Gulfside Wave-
land, Mississippi, 1927.

*Arthur P. Bedou, 1943-1963: On the Occasion
of His Retirement as First Vice-President.*
The People's Life Insurance Company of
Louisiana, February 22, 1963.

New Orleans States Item, June 3, 1966, p. 11.

BROWDER, B.B.
b. Knoxville, Tennessee; active 1900s.

Crisis, February 1915, p. 187. Browder, one
of Knoxville's leading photographers, was
known as the official photographer for the
Knoxville railroads.

CAMPBELL, JAMES S., PVT.
(dates unknown)

Campbell was a self-taught commercial photographer. He opened his first studio in Virginia
in 1915. During the First World War, Campbell
was the only black photographer commissioned
by the government to take photographs of camps
and army maneuvers. Upon moving to New York
after the war, Campbell opened a portrait
studio, "Campbell and Bennett," in Harlem.

PRINCIPAL SUBJECTS
World War I army camps, studio portraits.

PROCESS
Silver prints.

COLLECTIONS
National Archives, U.S. Army Signal Corps,
Washington, D.C.

SELECTED BIBLIOGRAPHY

*Exhibit of Fine Arts Production of American
Negro Artists.* Catalog describing exhibit
at the International House, New York, June
11, 1928.

COLLINS, HERBERT
Active in Boston, Massachusetts, 1900s.

Collins photographed Boston's black community
from the turn of the century through the
1920s. His photographs document the life
style of that community.

PRINCIPAL SUBJECTS
Portraits, street scenes.

PROCESS
Tintypes, silver prints.

COLLECTIONS
Coy M. LaSister, New York, New York.

African Meeting House, Boston, Massachusetts.

GANAWAY, KING DANIEL
(1883-?)

Ganaway practiced photography in Chicago
from 1914 through the 1930s. His subjects
ranged from the crowded waterways of the
Chicago River to the sentimental portraits
of family life and peasantry that occupied
many European painters in the late 19th and
early 20th centuries. His photographs roman-
ticized the industrialization of America
through a high contrast of light and shade
and through use of soft focus.

Ganaway's talent developed late in his life,
under peculiar circumstances. Arriving in
Chicago in 1914, he worked as a butler for
one of Chicago's wealthiest families and
soon thereafter became interested in the art
of photography. He was a serious student, and
spent all his spare time experimenting and
observing: "I see pictures and designs in
everything ... as I am riding on a streetcar,
I am constantly watching the changing lights
and shadows along the streets. Using the car
as a frame, I compose pictures...." However,
he felt that the subjects of his pictures
were uninteresting to other photographers.
Ganaway was not recognized in any of the
photographic journals or communities such
as Stieglitz's *Camera Work* and the Photo-
Secessionists, although his intent and style
aligned him with the pictorialist movement.

Ganaway's work did win him admirers, however.
In 1918, he received the first prize in the
John Wanamaker Annual Exhibition of photographs, and his work was shown frequently
with the Harmon Foundation annual exhibitions.
Recognition of his photographs in the Chicago
community eventually lead to a position with
a Chicago newspaper, *The Bee*. Additional exhibitions included the Texas Centennial in
1936 and the Museum of Science & Industry at
the New Jersey State Museum in 1935.

PRINCIPAL SUBJECTS
Architecture of Chicago and its environs,
portraits, and landscapes.

PROCESS
Silver prints.

COLLECTIONS
Library of Congress, Washington, D.C.

National Archive & Records Service, Harmon
Foundation Collection, Washington, D.C.

SELECTED BIBLIOGRAPHY

Lloyd, Edith M. "This Negro Butler Has Become
a Famous Photographer." *American Magazine*,
1925, pp. 56-58.

Art Institute of Chicago. *The Negro in Art
Week*, November 16-23, 1927.

Harmon Foundation. *Exhibition of Productions
by Negro Artists*. 1933.

Harmon Foundation. *Negro Artists*. 1935.

Texas Centennial Exposition. *Thumbnail
Sketches of Exhibiting Artists*. 1936.

Walker, Rosalyn. *A Resource Guide to the
Visual Arts of Afro-Americans*. South Bend,
Indiana: South Bend Community School Corp.,
1971.

MACBETH, ARTHUR LAIDLER
(1864-?)
Active in Charleston, South Carolina, Baltimore, Maryland, and Norfolk, Virginia.

Arthur L. Macbeth was born in Charleston, South
Carolina, and studied at the Avery Normal Institute there. He learned photography under Ger-
man, French, and American artists and chemists.

Macbeth opened his first studio in 1886 in Charleston. He later moved to Baltimore, Maryland in 1910 and opened a studio in Baltimore. About the same, he opened a studio in Norfolk, Virginia. It appears he had two studios operating at the same time. He was awarded medals and diplomas at the South Carolina Fair, 1890; Cotton States Exposition, Atlanta, Georgia, 1895; South Carolina Interstate and West Indian Exposition, Charleston, 1902; Jamestown Tercentennial Exposition, 1907, for his photographs. He was among the pioneers in motion pictures. He invented "Macbeth's Daylight Projecting Screen" for the purpose of showing stereoptican and moving pictures in daylight. In addition, Macbeth worked as the manager for the bureau of arts in the Negro Department of the South Carolina Interstate and West Indian Exposition, as a field agent and director of exhibits in the Negro Department of the Jamestown Exposition and was a member of the Photographers' Association of America.

SELECTED BIBLIOGRAPHY

Norfolk City Directory, 1909.

Who's Who of the Colored Race, Volume One, edited by Frank Lincoln, Publisher: Half-Century Anniversary of Negro Freedom in U.S., Chicago, 1915.

PROCESS
Silver gelatin prints.

SUBJECT
Portraits.

COLLECTIONS
Schomburg Center for Research in Black Culture, New York, New York.

SCURLOCK, ADDISON N.
(1883-1964)

Born in Fayetteville, North Carolina, Scurlock was active in photography from the early 1900s, when he became an apprentice at Rice Studios in Washington, D.C. He opened his first studio there in 1911, which he operated until 1964, with the assistance of his wife and later his two sons, Robert and George.

Scurlock was best known for his fine portrait studies of businessmen, political leaders, writers, artists, and other celebrities who frequented the Washington area. In addition to these studio portraits, Scurlock photographed cornerstone ceremonies, rallies, meetings and conventions, and Washington architecture, and he acted as the official photographer for Howard University. By the 1930s Scurlock had developed an interest in moving pictures and created weekly newsreels, featuring Washington events, that showed nightly at six theatres.

His work was published in magazines such as the *Messenger, Opportunity*, and *Crisis*, and was awarded a Gold Medal for Excellence at the Jamestown Exposition in 1907.

PRINCIPAL SUBJECTS
Portraits, celebrations, street scenes, conventions.

PROCESS
Silver prints.

COLLECTIONS

Corcoran Gallery of Art, Washington, D.C.

Library of Congress, Washington, D.C.

Moorland-Spingarn Research Center, Howard University, Washington, D.C.

Schomburg Center for Research in Black Culture, New York, New York.

Scurlock Studios, Washington, D.C.

SELECTED BIBLIOGRAPHY

Crisis, April 1911. Cover photograph.

Crisis, July 1911, p. 111.

Crisis, November 1911. Cover photograph.

Crisis, February 1912, p. 155.

Crisis, September 1913. Cover photograph.

Messenger, February 1925. Cover photograph.

Crisis, July 1926. Cover photograph.

The Tuskegee Messenger, January 31, 1931, p. 7, col. 3. "One of Washington's Best Studios is Negro Owned."

Brawley, Benjamin. *The Negro Genius*. New York: Dodd, Mead & Co., 1937. Includes photographs of Samuel Coleridge-Taylor, Roland Hayes, and W.E.B. DuBois.

The Corcoran Gallery of Art. *Addison N. Scurlock*. Catalog for Scurlock exhibition in Washington, D.C., June 19-August 26, 1976.

VAN DER ZEE, JAMES
(1886-1983)

Van Der Zee's photographs captured the spirit and life of Harlem for over 50 years. His interest in photography began when he was 12 years old in Lenox, Massachusetts; he experimented with unsophisticated equipment for several years and, after mastering the technique, began photographing his family and friends. In 1906 he moved from Lenox to New York City with the intent of becoming a musician (he played the piano and violin). Soon after arriving in New York, he met and married his first wife, Kate Brown, and moved to Phoebus, Virginia, for a short time. In his spare time he photographed the people of Phoebus and nearby Hampton. In 1907 he moved back to New York, worked as a musician, formed the Harlem Orchestra, and photographed occasionally.

Van Der Zee opened his first studio in 1916 on 135th Street, one of Harlem's busiest streets. During this period he made frequent trips to Lenox in order to photograph his family; these Lenox pictures comprise a major portion of his early work. His photographs imitated the styles of the impressionist painters and the pictorialists.

A few years later, he opened GGG studio at 272 Lenox Avenue with his second wife, Gaynella. Van Der Zee had a steady flow of customers-- women, children, soldiers, and families both black and white. Van Der Zee painted most of his own backdrops. He used a number of means to obtain a desired effect--hand tinting, multiple printing, and negative retouching. Regardless of whether the subjects were famous or unknown, all his photographs were given the same careful attention. During the 1920s, Van Der Zee often worked outside of the studio. As the official photographer for Marcus Garvey and the Universal Negro Improvement Association, he photographed their parades, conventions, rallies, and families. Noted also for his photographs of funerals, Van Der Zee began this practice around 1920 using an 8" x 10" camera.

Yet, with the advent of smaller cameras and

with more studios opening, his business dropped.
Only after a 25-year hiatus did Van Der Zee
begin photographing again, with the help of
his third wife, Donna. He reopened his studio
in 1980 and his most recent subjects were
Lou Rawls, Bill Cosby, and Eubie Blake.

PRINCIPAL SUBJECTS
Harlem street scenes, portraits, funerals.

PROCESS
Silver prints, hand tinting.

COLLECTIONS

Lunn Gallery, Washington, D.C.

Metropolitan Museum of Art, New York, New York.

Schomburg Center for Research in Black Culture,
New York, New York.

Studio Museum in Harlem, New York, New York.

James Van Der Zee personal collection, New
York, New York.

SELECTED BIBLIOGRAPHY
Newspapers and Magazines:

Ebony, October 1970, pp. 85-94.

Encore, Summer 1972, pp. 62-63.

Thornton, Gene. "Van Der Zee: Photographer
and Artist." *New York Times*, March 17, 1974.

Wittenberg, Clarissa K. "An Intimate Record
of how it was in Yesterday's Harlem." *Smith-
sonian*, June 1975, pp. 84-91.

Black World, February 1976, p. 49.

Mungen, Donna. "Portraits in Black." *Players*,
February 1976, pp. 38-42.

Fraser, C. Gerald. "Vanderzee Institute Gets
New Home." *New York Times*, June 6, 1976.

Parson, Ann. "Take The A Train." *Boston Phoenix*,
October 11, 1977.

Trebay, Guy. "James Van Der Zee at 92: Harlem
on his Mind." *Village Voice*, November 21,
1977, p. 77.

Drane, Francesca. "Memories in Black and
White." *New World*, March 24, 1978.

Tallmer, Jerry. "A Memory from Harlem."
New York Post, March 3, 1979.

"James Van Der Zee, New Life, New Wife at 94."
Ebony, May 1981, pp. 150-54.

Kodak Studio Light 1, 1982:20-24.

Berman, Avis, "James Van Der Zee" and "The
Picture Taking Man." *Boston Globe* (magazine
section), March 21, 1982, p. 12.

Lifson, Ben. "James Van Der Zee, Photographer."
Portfolio, March/April 1982, pp. 104-107.
"A self-taught photographer of intuitive
artistry, he recorded fifty years of life
in Harlem with a clear yet generous life
and a genius for pattern and light."

Books:

Schoener, Allon, ed. *Harlem on my Mind: Cultural Capital of Black America 1900-1968*.
New York: Random House, 1968.

The World of James Van Der Zee. Introduction
by Reginald McGhee. New York: Grove Press,
1969.

James Van Der Zee. Introduction by Regenia A.
Perry. Dobbs Ferry, New York: Morgan and
Morgan, 1973.

Alternative Center for International Arts.
James Van Der Zee. New York, 1977. Exhibition catalog.

Billops, Camille, and Dodson, Owen. *The Harlem
Book of the Dead: Photographs by James Van
Der Zee*. Dobbs Ferry, New York: Morgan and
Morgan, 1978.

ALLEN, JAMES LATIMER
(1907-1977)

Allen's interest in photography began in
grade school. As a member of a camera club
and an apprentice to a large illustrating
firm, Allen attained public recognition as
a skilled artist at an early age. He also
did commercial photography and published
regularly in *Opportunity, Crisis,* and the
Messenger.

Allen worked for a number of years as an
instructor for the WPA (Works Project Administration) Harlem Art Center. He was a prolific and well-known portrait photographer
in New York City in the 1920s and 1930s and
many members of the Harlem Renaissance sat
for him, including Alain Locke, Countee
Cullen, Langston Hughes, Claude McKay, and
Arthur Schomburg. In the 1930s, Locke described
Allen as being "by far the most outstanding
and promising young Negro in this modern
field of growing importance--art photography."

Allen exhibited at the Carnegie Institute,
Pittsburgh (1928), the Rotterdam Salon, London
(1929-30), Harmon Foundation Exhibits (1929,
1931, 1933), National Gallery of Art (1933),
Harmon Foundation College Art Association
Touring Exhibition (1934-35), and the Texas
Centennial Exposition (1936).

PRINCIPAL SUBJECTS
Portraits.

PROCESS
Silver prints.

COLLECTIONS
Library of Congress, Washington, D.C.

Moorland-Spingarn Research Center, Howard
University, Washington, D.C.

National Archives, Harmon Foundation, Washington, D.C.

Schomburg Center for Research in Black Culture,
New York, New York.

Yale University, James Weldon Johnson Memorial
Collection, New Haven, Connecticut.

SELECTED BIBLIOGRAPHY

Opportunity, December 1926, p. 369.

*Exhibit of Fine Arts Productions of American
   Negro Artists.* Catalog describing exhibit
   at the International House, New York, June
   17, 1928.

Art Digest, March 1, 1933, p. 18.

Harmon Foundation. *Catalog of Negro Artists,*
   1935.

Texas Centennial Exposition. *Thumbnail Sketches
   of Exhibiting Artists.* 1936.

Dover, Cedric. *AMERICAN NEGRO ART.* New York:
   New York Graphic Society, 1960, p. 31.

Harley, Ralph Jr. "Checklist of Afro-American
   Art and Artists." *The Serif,* December 1970.

BAKER, WALTER
New York, New York (active 1900-1930's)

Walter Baker owned a commercial studio in
Harlem. He photographed a number of prominent
community leaders and made portraits of his
neighbors. His photographs were exhibited
with the Harmon Foundation Fine Arts exhibits.

PRINCIPAL SUBJECTS
Portraits.

PROCESS
Silver prints.

COLLECTION
Schomburg Center for Research in Black Culture,
New York, New York.

SELECTED BIBLIOGRAPHY

Harmon Foundation, Exhibition of fine art
Productions of American Artists, "Photographic
Exhibit" (catalog) International House, New
York, January 6-17, 1928.

DeCARAVA, ROY
b. New York, 1919.
Active New York, 1940 to present.

DeCarava studied art at Cooper Union in New
York City, the Work Progress Administration's
Harlem Art Center, and the George Washington
Carver Art School. In the late 1940s he began
using his camera to record pictorial information for further study, e.g., silk screen
prints and paintings. By 1947 he was serious-
ly interested in photography as an art form
and, although he had little formal training
in photography, he studied books and the
works of other photographers. Also in 1947,
DeCarava began to use Harlem as the subject
of his art, making portraits of the people
and the streets. DeCarava later met Edward
Steichen, who suggested that he apply for a
Guggenheim scholarship, which he received the
next year. This grant of $3200 was the first
awarded to a black photographer. DeCarava
continued to make photographs of the black
residents and musicians of Harlem in their
homes, on the stoops, and in natural settings
for the next forty years.

DeCarava has worked as a photographer for
Sports Illustrated and currently teaches
photography at Hunter College, New York.

PRINCIPAL SUBJECTS
Harlem, its people and neighborhoods; musicians.

PROCESS
Silver prints.

COLLECTIONS

Andover Art Gallery, Andover-Phillips
Academy, Massachusetts.

Art Institute of Chicago, Chicago, Illinois.

Atlanta University, Atlanta, Georgia.

Belafonte Enterprises, Inc., New York.

Center for Creative Photography, University
of Arizona, Arizona.

The Corcoran Gallery of Art, Washington, D.C.

Harlem Art Collection, New York State Office
Building, New York.

Lee Witkin Gallery, New York.

Menil Foundation, Inc., Houston, Texas.

Metropolitan Museum of Fine Arts, Houston,
Texas.

The Museum of Fine Arts, Houston, Texas.

Museum of Modern Art, New York.

Olden Camera, New York.

Joseph E. Seagram & Sons, Inc., New York.

Sheldon Memorial Art Gallery, University of
Nebraska, Nebraska.

SELECTED BIBLIOGRAPHY
Newspapers and Magazines:

Harper's, April 1964.

*Black Creations: New York University Afro-
American Institute*, Fall 1972.

Books:

Kouwenhoven, John A. *The Columbia Historical
Portrait of New York*. New York: Doubleday &
Company, Inc., 1953.

Popular Photography Annual. Boston: Ziff-Davis
Publishing Co., 1953.

U.S. Camera Annual. U.S. Camera Publishing
Co., 1953.

Steichen, Edward. *The Family of Man*. New York:
Simon & Schuster, 1955.

DeCarava, Roy, and Hughes, Langston. *The Sweet
Flypaper of Life*. New York: Hill and Wang,
1955.

Hansberry, Lorraine. *The Movement*. New York:
Simon & Schuster, 1964.

Szarkowski, John. *The Photographer's Eye*.
New York: Museum of Modern Art, 1966.

*The John Simon Guggenheim Memorial Fellows in
Photography*. Philadelphia College of Art,
1966.

Allinder, Jim. *Roy DeCarava, Photographer*.
Lincoln: University of Nebraska Press, 1970.

Fax, Elton C. *Seventeen Black Artists*. New
York: Dodd, Mead & Co., 1973.

Szarkowski, John. *Looking at Photographs*.
New York: Museum of Modern Art, 1973.

Black Photographers Annual, Vol. 1. Brooklyn,
New York: Joe Crawford, 1973.

Black Photographers Annual, Vol. 2. Brooklyn,
New York, Joe Crawford, 1974.

Black Photographers Annual, Vol. 3. Brooklyn,
New York: Joe Crawford, 1975.

Short, Alvia Wardlaw. *Roy DeCarava: Photographs*. Houston: The Museum of Fine Arts,
1975.

Livingston, Jane, and Fralin, Frances. *Roy
DeCarava, The Nation's Capital in Photo-
graphs, 1976*. Washington, D.C.: Gallery of
Art, 1976.

Gee, Helen. *Photography of the Fifties*. New
York: Center for Creative Photography, 1980.

EXHIBITIONS

"Photographs." New York: Forty-Fourth Street
Gallery, 1950.

"Photographs." New York: New York Public
Library, 1951.

"Guggenheim Photographs." New York: New York
Public Library, 1954.

"DeCarava." A Photographer's Gallery, 1955.

"One Man Show." New York: Camera Club of
New York, 1956.

"Six Modern Masters." The IFA Galleries,
1958.

"US." New York: New York Public Library, 1967.

"Thru Black Eyes." New York: Studio Museum
in Harlem, 1969.

"Roy DeCarava: Photographs." University of
Nebraska, Lincoln: Sheldon Memorial Art
Center, 1970.

"Photographic Perspectives: Roy DeCarava."
University of Massachusetts, 1974.

"Roy DeCarava: Photographs." Houston: The
Museum of Fine Arts, 1975.

"Roy DeCarava: The Nation's Capitol in
Photographs." Washington, D.C.: Corcoran
Gallery of Art, 1976.

"Roy DeCarava: Photographs." Witkin Gallery,
1977.

"Roy DeCarava: Photographer." Friends of
Photography, 1980.

"Photography of the Fifties." New York:
Center for Creative Photography, 1980.

"The Sound I Saw: Jazz Photographs of Roy
DeCarava." Studio Museum of Harlem, 1983.

CLOUD, FRANK HERMAN
Active 1920s and 1930s.

Cloud was born in Miller's Ferry, Alabama,
on September 2, 1890. He attended Knoxville
College and Ohio State University and com-
pleted the Teacher's Course. However, he
decided to study photography with Vreeland,
a noted photographer in San Diego, California,
and subsequently opened his first studio in
Birmingham, Alabama. After living a time in
Cleveland, Ohio, he returned to California
in 1935 and opened a Los Angeles studio.
Cloud was noted for his photographs of children. (The information above was provided by
Mrs. Doris Cloud in a letter of September
23, 1982.)

Cloud's Children's Pictorial Magazine, 1936.

DuBois, W.E.B. *Brownies' Books*. New York:
DuBois and Dill Publishers, 1920.

ELCHA, EDDIE
Active in New York, New York, 1900-1930s.

Elcha photographed Harlem and its environs,
particularly the night clubs, chorus lines,
and entertainers. His work can be found in
the Schomburg Collection for Research in
Black Culture.

SELECTED BIBLIOGRAPHY

*The World of James Van Der Zee: A Visual
Record of Black Americans*. Compiled
by and Introduction by Reginald McGhee.
New York: Grove Press, 1969. Mentions
Elcha.

HANSEN, AUSTIN
(1910-)
Active 1930s to the present.

Hansen's career in photography began in
the Virgin Islands, where he was born. His
teacher was Clair Taylor, the Islands'
official photographer in the early 1920s.
In 1928 Hansen moved to New York City where
he took numerous jobs as messenger, elevator
operator, and musician. He played the drums
in the local clubs of Harlem and later,
during the WPA years, joined the musicians'
union which enabled him to play with larger
bands in clubs out of the city.

Also during the WPA years Hansen studied
art and began photographing more extensively
with the assistance of his brother, Aubrey.
In the Navy during World War II, he learned
combat/war photography. He was given the
rank of photographer's mate, 2nd class, and
he worked with the Office of War Information
in 1945.

After the war, Hansen moved back to Harlem
to set up the studio on West 135th Street
which he continues to occupy today. He is
noted for his photographs of the churches,
professional schools, organizations, personalities and events in Harlem, and his collection of over 20,000 photographs was recently donated to the Schomburg Center for
Research in Black Culture. His work has
appeared in the *Amsterdam News*, *New York Age*,
African Opinion, and *People's Voice*.

PRINCIPAL SUBJECTS
Street scenes, portraits.

PROCESS
Silver prints.

COLLECTIONS
Austin Hansen, private collection.

Schomburg Center for Research in Black
Culture, New York, New York.

SELECTED BIBLIOGRAPHY

Mitchell, Denise. "Harlem: Through the Eyes
   of Austin Hansen." (Source and date unidentified: article in the vertical file
   headed "Photography-Photographers," Schomburg Center.)

HARLESTON, ELISE FORREST
b. Charleston, South Carolina (1891-1970).

Harleston studied photography at Tuskegee
Institute, Alabama, with C.M. Battey in 1921.
She later opened a photographic studio with
her artist-husband, Edwin A. Harleston, who
had a painting studio on the top floor of
their home. "They opened the Harleston
Studio. He was the painter and she was
a photographer" (Edwina Whitlock in conversation with author, May 25, 1983). Many
of the portraits Edwin Harleston painted
were from Elise's photographic studies.

PRINCIPAL SUBJECTS
Portraits.

PROCESS
Silver prints.

COLLECTIONS
Edwina Harleston Whitlock, Charleston, South
Carolina.

HARRIS, FRANK
Philadelphia, Pennsylvania; active 1900-1930s.

Harris had one of the largest studios in
Philadelphia owned by an African American.
He photographed social clubs, cornerstone
layings, and the people of Philadelphia (both
black and white). His photographs are in the
private collection of Betty Lawrence, Philadelphia, Pennsylvania.

PRINCIPAL SUBJECTS
Portraits, street scenes.

PROCESS
Silver prints.

COLLECTIONS
Betty Lawrence, Philadelphia, Pennsylvania.

Schomburg Center for Research in Black Culture,
New York, New York.

Conversation with private collector, Betty
Lawrence, Philadelphia, Pennsylvania.

KEITH, DEWITT
b. Washington, D.C. (1923-1971).

During World War II, Keith was a photographer
for the Department of the Office of Strategic
Services. As a portrait photographer for the
Department of State, he made photographs of
many dignitaries, among them John Foster
Dulles, Herbert Hoover, Jr., Carter G. Woodson, and Claire Booth Luce. One of the portraits of John Foster Dulles was reproduced
on a four-cent U.S. postage stamp in 1960.
Keith also worked as a freelance and jour-
nalistic photographer and he taught photography at the Capitol School of Photography
in Washington, D.C. (The information above
was provided by Mrs. Doris T. Keith in a
letter of February 2, 1981.)

Farber, John. "The Quest to Honor Photographers
   of Photo Postage Stamp." *Photographica*,
   Volume XIII, No. 2 (Photographic Historical
   Society of New York), February 1981, p. 5.

McNEILL, ROBERT
b. Washington, D.C.; active 1930s.

McNeill is noted for his photographs of the
Roosevelt administration, particularly the
"Black Cabinet," and the National Youth Ad-
ministration, a work incentive program headed
by Mary McCloud Bethune. A graduate of the
New York Institute of Photography, he was
appointed photographic consultant for the
Works Progress Administration.

COLLECTIONS
Library of Congress, Washington, D.C.

National Archives and Records Service,
Washington, D.C.

Schomburg Center for Research in Black Culture, New York, New York.

MERCER, R.E.
Active in New York, New York, 1900-1930s.

SELECTED BIBLIOGRAPHY

Harmon Foundation. Exhibition of Fine Art
Productions of American Artists, "Photo-

graphic Exhibit" (catalog) International House, New York, January 6-17, 1928.

Mercer worked in three of New York's leading photographic studios in the 1920s. Many of his photographs chronicled the life and activities of businesswoman Mme C.J. Walker and her daughter A'Leila Walker.

COLLECTIONS
A'Leila Bundles, Atlanta, Georgia.

Schomburg Center for Research in Black Culture, New York, New York.

PARKS, GORDON
b. Kansas City (1912-).
Active 1930s to the present.

Parks left Kansas City at the age of sixteen, making his way to Minneapolis and later to Chicago. He worked as a piano player, busboy, dining car waiter, and professional basketball player. In 1937, he decided that he wanted to be a photographer after seeing the works of the Farm Security Administration photographers and viewing a newsreel of Japanese planes bombing targeted areas. He was later hired by Roy Stryker of the F.S.A. as a photographer; during World War II he worked as an Office of War Information correspondent and, after the war, as a photographer for the Standard Oil Company in New Jersey. In 1949 he became a staff photographer for *Life* and was quite active covering stories of the Black Muslims, the story of a Brazilian boy named Flavio, and life in the black neighborhoods in America until 1972. Additionally, he has worked as a composer, filmmaker, painter, and writer.

PRINCIPAL SUBJECTS
Farm Security Administration photographs, street scenes, portraits.

PROCESS
Silver prints, color photography.

COLLECTIONS
Library of Congress, Washington, D.C.

Life, New York.

Schomburg Center for Research in Black Culture, New York, New York.

SELECTED BIBLIOGRAPHY
Newspapers and Magazines:

Negro Digest, January 1944, pp. 41-42.

Ebony, July 1946, pp. 24-29.

Ebony, December 1957, p. 134.

Tuesday, September 1967, p. 11.

Life, March 8, 1968, p. 3.

Life, November 15, 1968, pp. 116-124.

Detroit Free Press, August 17, 1969, p. B-6.

Washington Post, September 27, 1969 (Film section).

Crisis, July 1971, p. 162.

New York Times, July 25, 1971, p. D-13.

Detroit Free Press, November 14, 1971, p. 12.

Black Collegian, January/February 1972, p. 15.

Essence, October 1972, p. 62.

Encore, November 3, 1975, pp. 31-33.

Books:

Toppin, Edgar A. *A Biographical History of Blacks in America Since 1528*. New York: McKay, 1971.

Cederholm, Theresa D. *Afro-American Artists*. Trustees of the Boston Public Library, 1973.

Landay, Eileen. *Black Film Stars*. New York: Drake Publishers, 1973.

Shockley, Ann A., and Chandler, Sue P. *Living Black American Authors--A Biographical Directory*. New York: R.R. Bowker & Co., 1973.

Bogle, Donald. *Toms, Coons, Bucks, and Mulattoes*. New York: Viking Press, 1973.

Rush, Theressa G. *Black American Writers Past and Present*. Metuchin, New Jersey: Scarecrow Press, 1975. Vol. 2.

Negro Almanac. New York: Bellwether Publishers, 1976.

PHIPPS, EDGAR EUGENE
(1887-)

Phipps was born in Kingston, Jamaica, and later moved to New York City, where he set up a studio. He photographed theatrical personalities in the New York area during the 1920s and early 1930s. In addition, he had a successful business taking portraits in the local Harlem community. In 1933 Phipps exhibited with the Harmon Foundation in New York and at Buckingham Palace, and in 1979 one of his photographs was featured in the International Center for Photography's (New York) exhibition, "Fleeting Gestures: Treasures of Dance Photography."

PRINCIPAL SUBJECTS
Portraits.

PROCESS
Silver gelatin prints.

COLLECTIONS
National Archives, Records, and Research Service, Harmon Foundation Collection, Washington, D.C.

Schomburg Center for Research in Black Culture, New York, New York.

BIBLIOGRAPHY

"Exhibit of Fine Arts: Production of American Negro Artists." New York: Harmon Foundation, 1935. Catalog.

POLK, P.H.
(1898-)
b. Tuskegee, Alabama.

Polk studied photography at Tuskegee Institute under C.M. Battey and was apprenticed in Chicago to the black photographer, Fred Jensen. Like many photographers, Polk had originally wanted to be a painter.

Polk opened his first studio in Tuskegee in 1927. In 1928, he was appointed to the faculty of the Tuskegee Institute's Photography Department. Later, Polk became head of that photography department and Tuskegee's official photographer. He photographed visitors to the Institute such as Mary McCloud Bethune, Paul

Robeson, Eleanor Roosevelt, and the renowned Tuskegee scientist George Washington Carver. Polk's work also depicts the life style of the people of the area.

"Mr. Polk was and is interested in recording what he sees around him and what he sees within his own head and his own heart and that is what he has done" (Pearl Lomax from portfolio on Polk, 1980).

PRINCIPAL SUBJECTS
Portraits.

PROCESS
Silver prints.   _

COLLECTIONS
Library of Congress, Washington, D.C.

Nexus Gallery, Atlanta, Georgia.

P.H. Polk Collection, Photographer's Collection, Tuskegee, Alabama.

Schomburg Center for Research in Black Culture, New York, New York.

Tuskegee Institute, Tuskegee, Alabama.

EXHIBITIONS

Art Institute of Pittsburgh, Pittsburgh, Pennsylvania. (date unknown)

Corcoran Gallery, Washington, D.C., 1981.

House of Friendship, Soviet Union. (date unknown)

Museum of National History, New York, New York. (date unknown)

Studio Museum in Harlem, New York, New York, 1979.

Washington Gallery, Washington, D.C., 1981.

SELECTED BIBLIOGRAPHY

Black Photographers Annual, Vol. 2. Brooklyn, New York: Joe Crawford, 1974. Includes portfolio. "P.H. Polk ... a kind of general practitioner."

New York Times, January 14, 1980. "A Photographer, 81, is Honored for 50 Years of Work."

Lomax, Pearl. *P.H. Polk*. Atlanta: Nexus Press, 1980.

Lomax, Pearl. *P.H. Polk Portfolio*. Atlanta: Southlight, 1981. Limited edition of 11 photographs accompanied by written commentary.

Thornton, Gene. "P.H. Polk's Genius Versus Modernism." *New York Times*, February 2, 1982.

POOLE, PAUL
Active in Atlanta, Georgia, 1900-1940.

Poole is most noted for his photographs of the black community in Atlanta.

COLLECTION
Atlanta Historical Society, Atlanta, Georgia.

ROBERTS, RICHARD SAMUEL
b.1881-1936.
Active in Fernandina, Florida, and Columbia, South Carolina.

Richard S. Roberts worked as a stevedore, later as a custodian at the Fernandina, Florida, post office. He began studying photography through correspondence courses and books and opened his first studio in his home in Fernandina with the assistance of his wife, Wilhelmina Williams Roberts. Roberts moved to Columbia, South Carolina, and opened a larger studio in the downtown area of Columbia. He continued to work at night as a custodian in the post office in Columbia. He advertised that his studio took superior photographs by day or by night. "To those who desire photographs made of parents and grandparents but can't persuade them to visit the studio, we say:--Leave them at home. They probably love their home surroundings. Engage us to make that sitting at home. We will respond with pleasure."

Roberts, with his wife acting as assistant, travelled throughout the state of South Carolina in the 1920s and 1930s, photographing church groups, schools, and community organizations. He also made portraits of the dead for family members. Roberts operated the *Roberts' Studio* until his death in 1936.

Letter to the author from his daughter, Wilhelmina, September 30, 1983.

South Carolina City Directory.

PROCESS
Silver gelatin prints, glass plate negatives.

PRINCIPAL SUBJECTS
Portraits, groups.

COLLECTIONS
Schomburg Center for Research in Black Culture, New York, New York.

Wilhelmina Wynn, private collection, New York, New York.

Carolinaian Library, Columbia, South Carolina.

SMITH, FRANK G.
Active in Los Angeles, California, 1930s.

Los Angeles News, April 10, 1930, p. 4, col. 3.

SMITH, MARVIN AND MORGAN
(1910-)
Active New York, 1930s-1950s.

Twin brothers Marvin and Morgan Smith were prolific photographers in Harlem in the 1930s and 1940s. Their studio, located near the Apollo Theater on 125th Street, was frequented by performing artists, writers, historians, and others of the Harlem community. Their cameras captured the Lindy Hoppers in the Savoy Ballroom and Easter Sunday in Harlem as well as the political rallies, street corner preachers, and the breadlines during the Depression.

Marvin, also a successful painter during the WPA, worked as a photographer's mate, 3rd class, and as Chief Photographer's Mate in the Navy in World War II. He was the first black American to attend the Naval Air Station School of Photography and Motion Pictures at Pensacola, Florida. His paintings won 2nd prize in the Federal Art Exhibit in 1934 and 3rd prize in the Art Exhibit in 1940.

During the WPA Art Program, Morgan assisted muralist Vertis Hayes on the murals at Harlem Hospital Nurses' residence. In 1937 his photographs of a little boy playing paddle ball won first prize in the *Herald Tribune* contest.

The Smiths studied art in France in 1939, formed a newspaper picture service, and did pictorial editorials of Harlem and its leaders for the Urban League, *Ebony*, *Pittsburgh Courier*, *Crisis*, *Our World*, *Opportunity*, and *Travel Guide*. During the 1950s, the Smith twins also worked as sound and recording engineers for local TV stations. Their photographs have been included in Claude McKay's *Harlem Matropolis*, 1940. Over 30 photographs were included in an exhibit at the Schomburg Center's exhibition "Black Dance in Photographs, from the mid-19th Century to the Present" (1982), and 15 photographs were part of Tom Beck's 1982 exhibition entitled "Blacks in Labor: 1850-1950" at the University of Maryland Library. In 1982 an organization in New York comprised of contemporary photographers--The International Black Photographers--honored the twins for their excellence and contributions to photography. The Smiths donated 2,000 of their photographs to the Schomburg Center's Photography Collection.

PRINCIPAL SUBJECTS
Harlem street scenes, portraits of authors, poets, performing and visual artists, historians, educators, and political figures.

PROCESS
Silver prints.

BIBLIOGRAPHY

Who's Who in Colored America. Yonkers, New York: Christian E. Burckel and Assoc., 1950.

Trottman, Beresford. *Who's Who in Harlem*. New York: Magazine & Periodical Printing & Publishing Co., Inc., 1950.

SPIGNER, W.H.S.
Active in Los Angeles, California, 1900-1920s.

Crisis, August 1913, p. 196.

Los Angeles New Age, April 2, 1915, p. 2.

STEPHENS, WALTER J.
Active in Syracuse, New York, 1930s.

Opportunity, February 1939.

WEBB, MILES
Active in Chicago, Illinois, 1900.

Crisis, December 1912. Advertisement for Webb's School of Photography; offers amateur, intermediate, and professional courses in all branches of photography.

Crisis, November 1913. Advertisement. "Webb. Chicago's Expert Photographer. I specialize in every phase of artistic picture making."

WEEMS, ELLIS L.
Active in Jacksonville, Florida, 1920-1960s.

Upon completing photography courses at Tuskegee Institute, Alabama, in 1922, Weems worked as a photographer's assistant in one of Atlanta's largest commercial and portrait photographic studios. In 1929, he opened his own studio in Jacksonville, Florida, and since that time has amassed over 300,000

prints and negatives of the people of Jacksonville. Weems has been a member of the Professional Photographers Association of America, Florida's Professional Photographers and the Southeastern Photographers Association since 1934. Weems also studied photography at the Winona Graduate School of Photography in Winona Lake, Indiana.

WOODARD STUDIOS
Active Chicago, Illinois, and Kansas City, Kansas, 1920s-1930s.

Messenger, October 1926. Advertisement including photograph. "The high quality of Woodward's photographs is notably attested by the large number of prominent men and women in the social, theatrical, commercial and political life of both Chicago and Kansas City, who prefer their distinctiveness...."

The following bibliography includes some of the
books, catalogues and films used in compiling
Black Photographers, 1840-1940.

BOOKS and CATALOGUES:

de Abajian, James T. *Blacks in Selected Newspapers, Censuses and Other Sources, An Index to Names and Subjects.* Boston: G.K.
Hall and Co., 1974.

*Arthur P. Bedou, 1943-1963: On the Occasion
of His Retirement as First Vice-President.*
The People's Life Insurance Company of
Louisiana, February 22, 1963.

Barthes, Roland. *Camera Lucida, Reflections
on Photography.* Translated by Richard
Howard. Toronto, Canada: McGraw-Hill,
Ryerson, Ltd., 1980.

Bearden, Romare, and Henderson, Harry. *Six
Black Masters of American Art.* New York:
Zenith Books, 1972.

Billops, Camille, and Dodson, Owen. *The
Harlem Book of the Dead: Photographs by
James Van Der Zee.* Dobbs Ferry, New York:
Morgan and Morgan, 1978.

Brawley, Benjamin. *The Negro Genius.* New York:
Dodd, Mead and Co., 1937.

Cederholm, Theresa D., ed. *Afro-American
Artists: A Bio-Bibliographical Directory.*
Boston: Trustees of the Boston Public
Library, 1973.

Dabney, Wendell P. *Cincinnati's Colored Citizens.* Cincinnati, Ohio: Dabney Publishing
Company, 1926.

Darrah, William Culp. *Stereoviews: A History
of Stereographs in America and Their Collections.* Gettysburg, Pennsylvania: Darrah,
1977.

Delaney, Martin R. *The Condition, Elevation,
Emigration and Destiny of the Colored
People of the United States.* Philadelphia:
privately printed, 1852.

Dover, Cedric. *American Negro Art.* Greenwich,
Connecticut: New York Graphic Society, 1960.

DuBois, W.E.B. *Negro Artisan.* Atlanta,
Georgia: Atlanta University Press, 1902.

————. *Negro American Artisan.* Atlanta,
Georgia: Atlanta University Press, 1913.

Gernsheim, Helmut, and Gernsheim, Allison.
A Concise History of Photography. New York:
Grosset and Dunlap, 1965.

Grimke, Charlotte Forten. *The Journal of
Charlotte L. Forten.* New York: Dryden Press,
1953.

Gulfside Association. *Pictures of Scenes and
Activities, the Journal, Eighth Annual
Meeting of the New Orleans Area Council.*
A scrapbook, conducted for Negroes by the
Department of Rural Work, Board of Home
Missions and Church extension Methodist
Episcopal Church, 1927.

*Harlem Heyday: The Photography of James Van
Der Zee.* New York: Studio Museum in Harlem,
1982.

Harmon Foundation. "Exhibition of Fine Art
by American Negro Artists." Arranged in
cooperation with the Commission on the
Church and Race Relations, Federal Council
of Churches. New York: International House,
1928-1935.

Harmon Foundation. "Exhibition of Productions
by Negro Artists." New York: International
House, 1933.

Harmon Foundation. *Negro Artists: An Illustrated Review of Their Achievements.* New
York: International House, 1935.

*The Historic Photographs of Addison N. Scur-
lock.* Washington, D.C.: Corcoran Gallery
of Art, 1974.

Jackson, Giles B., and Davis, D. Webster.
*The Industrial History of the Negro Race
of the United States.* Richmond, Virginia:
Negro Educational Association, 1911.

James Van Der Zee. Dobbs Ferry, New York:
Morgan and Morgan, 1973.

Life Library of Photography. *The Camera:
Caring for Photographs; Frontiers of
Photography.* New York: Time, Inc., 1972.

Locke, Alain. *Negro Art: Past and Present.*
Washington, D.C.: Associates in Negro
Folk Education, 1936.

McGhee, Reginald. *The World of James Van Der
Zee.* New York: Morgan and Morgan, 1973.

McKay, Claude. *Harlem: Negro Metropolitan.*
New York: E.P. Dutton and Co., 1940.

Newhall, Beaumont. *The Daguerreotype in
America.* New York: Duell, Sloan & Pearce,
1961.

————. *The History of Photography.* New
York: Museum of Modern Art, 1964.

New Orleans City Directory.

Perry, Regenia A. *Selections of Nineteenth
Century Afro-American Art.* New York:
Metropolitan Museum of Art, 1976.

P.H. Polk. Atlanta, Georgia: Nexus Press,
1980.

Porter, James A. *Ten Afro-American Artists.*
Washington, D.C.: Howard University Gallery
of Art, 1967.

Richmond City Directory.

Rinhart, Floyd, and Rinhart, Marion. *American
Daguerrean Art.* New York: Clarkson Potter,
1967.

Rudisill, Richard. *Mirror Image: The Influ-
ence of the Daguerreotype in American
Society.* Albuquerque: University of New
Mexico Press, 1971.

Schoener, Allon, ed. *Harlem on My Mind:
Cultural Capitol of Black America 1900-
1968.* New York: Random House, 1968.

Simmons, William J. *Men of Mark.* Cleveland,
Ohio: G.M. Rewell and Company, 1887.

Texas Centennial Exposition. "Thumbnail
Sketches of Exhibiting Artists." Dallas,
Texas, 1936.

Thompson, Lucille Smith. *The Negro in Montana
1800-1945.*

Two Centuries of Black American Art. David
Driskell, travelling exhibition curator,
Los Angeles County Museum. New York: Alfred
A. Knopf, 1976.

Walker, Rosalyn. *A Resource Guide to the Visual Arts of Afro-Americans*. South Bend, Indiana: South Bend Community School Corp., 1971.

Weinstein, Robert A., and Booth, Larry. *Collection, Use and Care of Historical Photographs*. Nashville, Tennessee: American Association for State and Local History, 1977.

Weisendanger, Martin, and Weisendanger, Margaret. *Nineteenth Century Louisiana Painters from the Collection of W.E. Grove*. Gretona, Louisiana: Pelican, 1971.

Williams, George W. *Negro Race in America*. New York: G.R. Putnam's Sons, 1883.

FILMS:

Uncommon Images: James Van Der Zee at 91. WNBC-TV, New York, New York.

Interview with James Van Der Zee. Dick Cavett Show, Public Broadcasting System (PBS), New York, New York.

The Photographs

Photographer: J.P. Ball & Son, Montana. Inscribed on verso "Beatrice, from Gladys."
Albumen print, ca. 1880. Schomburg Center for Research in Black Culture, NYPL. Clarence Cameron White Collection.

Photographer: Jules Lion. Unidentified black man. Tintype, ca. 1850.
Anonymous collection, New York.

Photographer: Augustus Washington. Unidentified portrait of a young boy. Daguerreotype, ca. 1842. Schomburg Center for Research in Black Culture, NYPL.

Photographer: James Conway Farley. George W. Davis studio. John Smith, minister to Liberia. Albumen print, cabinet card, 1880. Schomburg Center for Research in Black Culture, NYPL.

Photographer: James Conway Farley. George W. Davis studio. Unidentified portrait of a woman. Albumen print, carte-de-visite, ca. 1870. Schomburg Center for Research in Black Culture, NYPL.

Photographer: A.S. Thomas, Cincinnati, Ohio. Unidentified portrait, ca. 1860s. Albumen print, carte-de-visite. Schomburg Center for Research in Black Culture, NYPL.

Photographer: Ball and Thomas, Cincinnati, Ohio. Unidentified portrait, ca. 1860s. Albumen print, carte-de-visite. Schomburg Center for Research in Black Culture, NYPL.

Photographer: Daniel Freeman. Gwendolyn Bennett. Silver gelatin print, ca. 1900. Schomburg Center for Research in Black Culture, NYPL. Gwendolyn Bennett Collection.

Photographer: Goodridge Brothers. Unidentified. Albumen print on cabinet card, ca. 1880s. Private collection, John V. Jezierski, Saginaw, MI.

Photographer: Goodridge Brothers. Unidentified. Albumen print on cabinet card, ca. 1880s. Private collection, John V. Jezierski, Saginaw, MI.

Photographer: Goodridge Brothers. Genesee Street Bridge after the Flood of 1870. Albumen print. Eddy Historical Collection, Hoyt Public Library, Saginaw, MI.

Photographer: Goodridge Brothers. High Water Near the Fire Tower after the Flood of April 1870. Albumen print. Eddy Historical Collection.

Photographer: Goodridge Brothers, Saginaw, MI. Scenes in the Pineries of Michigan. Albumen print, mounted stereographic photographs. Art, prints and photographs, NYPL. Robert Dennis Collection.

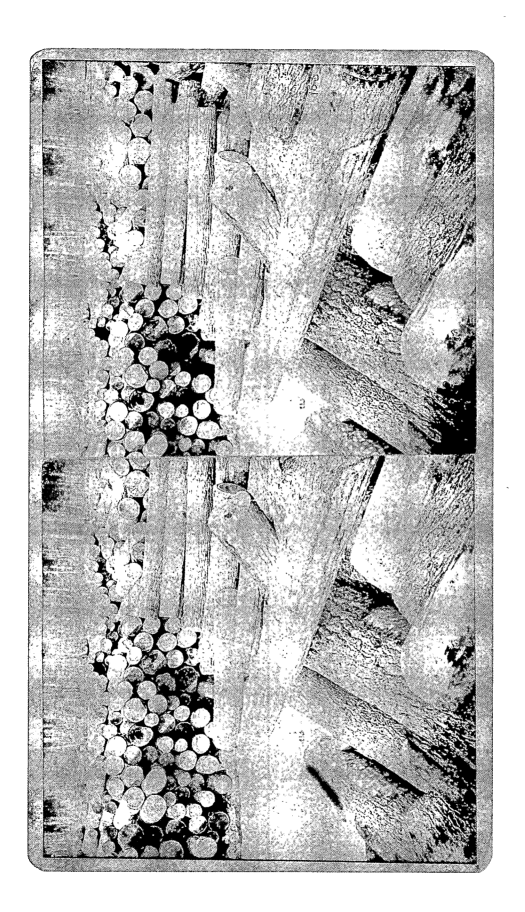

Photographer: Goodridge Brothers, Saginaw, MI. Ruins of Jackson Hall, South Washington Avenue, 1873. Albumen print, mounted stereographic photograph. Eddy Historical Collection, Hoyt Public Library, Saginaw, MI.

Photographer: Arthur Macbeth, Baltimore. George Freeman Bragg, DD. Albumen print, ca. 1910. Schomburg Center for Research in Black Culture, NYPL. George Freeman Bragg Collection.

Photographer: Arthur Macbeth, Norfolk. Unidentified portrait of a man. Albumen print, ca. 1900. Schomburg Center for Research in Black Culture, NYPL.

Photographer: Arthur Macbeth, Baltimore. Unidentified portrait of a rural church and its members. Albumen print, ca. 1900. Schomburg Center for Research in Black Culture, NYPL. George Freeman Bragg Collection.

"Our Heroes of Destiny"

Honorables
Frederick Douglass
John M. Langston
Blanche K. Bruce
Paul Laurence Dunbar and
Booker T. Washington

A genuine photogravure, printed on the finest grade of Japan-vellum, 20 x 25 inches in size, finished in Vandyke brown, embracing the master techniques of the engraver's and printer's crafts.

A photogravure is printed from a hand-tooled intaglio plate, and consists of fine particles of ink standing above the surface of the paper sufficiently to cast minute shadows. The depth of the ink and shadows cast by it give a richness to a photogravure impression which is absolutely unattainable by relief or planographic printing as done by half-tone, photo-gelatine, lithographic, or other similar processes. A perfect photogravure is the acme of the engraver's handicraft.

In publishing this valuable edition of these five notable men, I have gone to large expense in an endeavor to present to my race a rare etching of the highest technique possible to create. Price ONE DOLLAR. Send in your order now to

C. M. BATTEY
ARTIST and PUBLISHER.
322 Mott Ave., N. Y. City

This illustration is protected by copyright. Any infringement will be prosecuted.

"OUR HEROES OF DESTINY"

TESTIMONIALS

Dr. Booker T. Washington, Tuskegee Institute, Ala., says:

"I am really surprised, as well as gratified, at the fine piece of work you have gotten out. I had no idea you were going to get up such an artistic production, that is so attractive and so creditable."

The New York *Age*, New York City, says:

"Every home and classroom should honor one of these portraits, and into the mind of every child it should be grafted with the lines from the immortal poem of Longfellow: 'Lives of great men all remind us, we can make our lives sublime.'"

Dr. York Russell, New York City, says:

"Your artistic production of 'Our Heroes of Destiny' is unquestionably the master composition which has thus far chronicled the advent in perpetuating faithful likenesses of our hero-pioneers. The other nine series with which you propose to follow this will establish a precedent that will be of historic value in future years for yet unborn generations."

Rev. Dr. Reverdy C. Ransom, New York City, says:

"Your splendid production of 'Our Heroes of Destiny' marks the era of perpetuating characteristic and faithful likenesses of the famous men and women of our own race, to be handed down to younger generations, inspiring them with ideals which if carefully nurtured in their young lives will in their mature ages prove excellent examples of pure and dignified manhood and womanhood.

"No home where there is a child should be without a copy of this excellent work, and no parent that feels the love and loyalty of higher race development should fail to teach the children of their homes the meaning of the lives of these five men."

Major Charles R. Douglass, Washington, D. C., says:

"The likenesses and character blending in the selected gravure portraits of the group of 'Honorables' are better than any I have yet seen; and to those of our race who cherish the memories of these men they will be eagerly sought."

Mrs. B. K. Bruce, Washington, D. C., says:

"I am indeed glad to say that 'Our Heroes of Destiny' is the most creditable work of art that has yet been produced of and for our people. The life likeness of the entire group is exceedingly good. It is a fitting memorial worthy to be in every home.

"If we are to perpetuate the memories of our own great men, it must be by keeping their portraits ever before our youth, and familiarizing them with the true meaning of their lives."

AGENTS WANTED

Photographer: C.M. Battey. Advertisement in *The Crisis Magazine*, December 1915.

Photographer: C.M. Battey. Booker T. Washington. Silver gelatin print, 1915. Schomburg Center for Research in Black Culture, NYPL.

Photographer: C.M. Battey. Bob Cole and J. Rosamond Johnson. Platinum print, 1915. Schomburg Center for Research in Black Culture, NYPL.

Photographer: C.M. Battey. Unidentified portrait. Silver gelatin print, ca. 1920. Schomburg Center for Research in Black Culture, NYPL.

Dr. W. E. Burghardt DuBois   Paul Laurence Dunbar

Photographer: C.M. Battey. Silver gelatin print—post cards. Schomburg Center for Research in Black Culture, NYPL.

Hon. Frederick Douglass

Dr. Robert Russa Moton

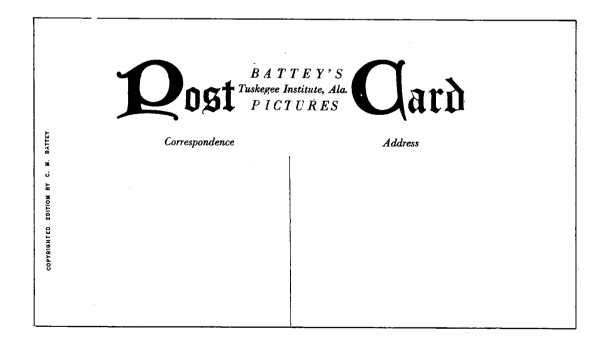

Photographer: C.M. Battey. Thomas Jesse Jones. Silver gelatin print, ca. 1920. Schomburg Center for Research in Black Culture, NYPL. Phelps-Stokes Collection.

Photographer: C.M. Battey. Tuskegee Institute students in carpentry. Silver gelatin print, ca. 1920. Schomburg Center for Research in Black Culture, NYPL. Phelps-Stokes Collection.

Photographer: C.M. Battey. Tuskegee Institute, Dressmaking class. Silver gelatin print, ca. 1920. Schomburg Center for Research in Black Culture, NYPL. Phelps-Stokes Collection.

Photographer: Arthur Bedou. President Taft receiving standing ovation. Silver gelatin print, ca. 1910. Schomburg Center for Research in Black Culture, NYPL.

Photographer: Arthur Bedou. Photographer in center of a large crowd. Silver gelatin print, ca. 1910. Schomburg Center for Research in Black Culture, NYPL.

Photographer: Arthur Bedou, New Orleans. Portrait of a woman. Silver gelatin print, ca. 1920. Schomburg Center for Research in Black Culture, NYPL.

Photographer: Arthur Bedou, New Orleans. Men playing croquet under the great oak trees, Mississippi. Silver gelatin print, ca. 1930. Schomburg Center for Research in Black Culture, NYPL.

Photographer: Arthur Bedou. Picnic at Gulfside, Mississippi. Silver gelatin print, ca. 1930. Schomburg Center for Research in Black Culture, NYPL.

Photographer: Addison Scurlock. President Roosevelt (laying of cornerstone at the colored YMCA, 12th Street, Washington, D.C., Thanksgiving Day, 1908). Silver gelatin print. Schomburg Center for Research in Black Culture, NYPL. Jesse Alexander, YMCA Collection.

Photographer: Addison Scurlock. Ernest Just. Silver gelatin print, 1915. Schomburg Center for Research in Black Culture, NYPL.

Photographer: Addison Scurlock. Vaudeville stars: Sunshine Sammy and Bro. Silver gelatin print, ca. 1915. Schomburg Center for Research in Black Culture, NYPL. Lawrence Jordan Collection.

Photographer: Addison Scurlock. Richard T. Greener. Silver gelatin print, ca. 1915. Schomburg Center for Research in Black Culture, NYPL.

Photographer: Addison Scurlock. Samuel Coleridge Taylor. Silver gelatin print, 1915. Schomburg Center for Research in Black Culture, NYPL.

Photographer: Addison Scurlock. Fredi Washington. Silver gelatin print, ca. 1930. Schomburg Center for Research in Black Culture, NYPL. Fredi Washington Collection.

Photographer: Addison Scurlock. White House Conference Group of the National Women's Council. Silver gelatin print, 1938. Schomburg Center for Research in Black Culture, NYPL.

Photographer: James Van Der Zee. "Daydreams." Silver gelatin print, ca. 1920. Collection of Donna Mussenden-Van Der Zee.

Photographer: James Van Der Zee. Garveyite Family portrait. Silver gelatin print, ca. 1920s. Schomburg Center for Research in Black Culture, NYPL. James Van Der Zee Collection.

Photographer: James Van Der Zee. Family portrait. Silver gelatin print, 1931. Schomburg Center for Research in Black Culture, NYPL. James Van Der Zee Collection.

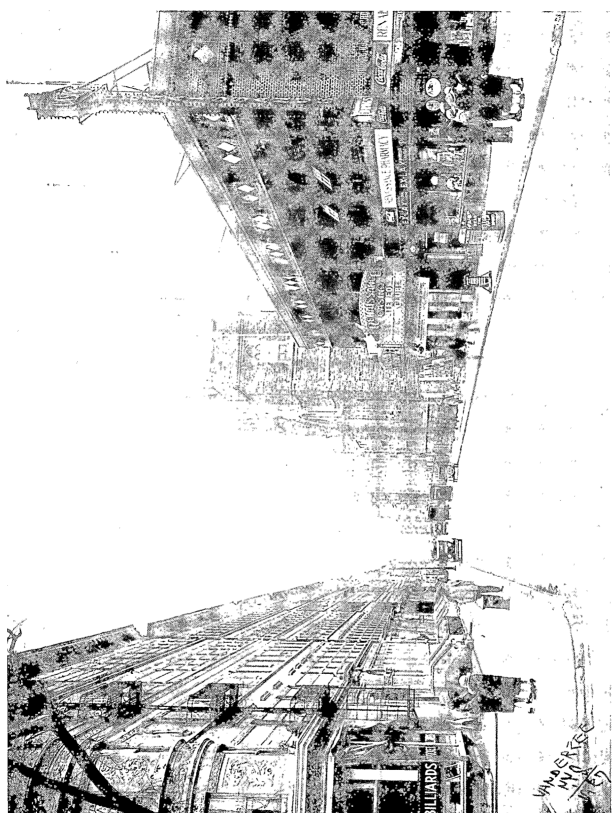

Photographer: James Van Der Zee. Renaissance Casino. Silver gelatin print, ca. 1927. Collection of Donna Mussenden–Van Der Zee.

Photographer: James Van Der Zee. Schomburg Reading Room. Silver gelatin print, 1928. Schomburg Center for Research in Black Culture, NYPL. James Van Der Zee Collection.

Photographer: James Van Der Zee. Portrait of violinist. Silver gelatin print, ca. 1930s. Schomburg Center for Research in Black Culture, NYPL. Shelton Family Collection.

Photographer: James Van Der Zee. Unidentified group of young boys in studio. Silver gelatin print, ca. 1930. Schomburg Center for Research in Black Culture, NYPL. James Van Der Zee Collection.

Photographer: James Van Der Zee. Pond Lily Club. Silver gelatin print, 1934. Schomburg Center for Research in Black Culture, NYPL. James Van Der Zee Collection.

Photographer: James Van Der Zee. Couple in raccoon coats. Silver gelatin print, 1932. Collection of Donna Mussenden–Van Der Zee.

Photographer: James Van Der Zee. Lester Walton. Silver gelatin print, 1932. Schomburg Center for Research in Black Culture, NYPL. Lester A. Walton Collection.

Photographer: James Van Der Zee. Eubie Blake. 1981. Collection of Donna Mussenden–Van Der Zee.

Photographer: Herbert Collins. Picnic on Boston Commons. Silver gelatin print, ca. 1910–1920. Collection of Coy Lasister, New York.

Photographer: Herbert Collins, Boston. Unidentified portrait. Silver gelatin print, ca. 1920. Collection of Coy Lasister, New York.

Photographer: Herbert Collins, Boston. Unidentified portrait of man in chair.
Silver gelatin print, ca. 1920. Collection of Coy Lasister, New York.

Photographer: Miles Webb. Woman on cover of *The Crisis Magazine*. Silver gelatin print, 1913. Schomburg Center for Research in Black Culture, NYPL.

Photographer: Frank Harris. William King. Silver gelatin print, 1920. Schomburg Center for Research in Black Culture, NYPL. Lawrence Brown Collection.

Photographer: R.E. Mercer. Harry D. Evans. Silver gelatin print, ca. 1920. Schomburg Center for Research in Black Culture, NYPL. Madame C.J. Walker Collection.

Photographer: R.E. Mercer. James Reese Europe and the Clef Club Band. Silver gelatin print, 1914. Schomburg Center for Research in Black Culture, NYPL.

Photographer: R.E. Mercer. Freeman Briley. Gelatin silver print, ca. 1920. Schomburg Center for Research in Black Culture, NYPL. Madame C.J. Walker Collection.

Photographer: R.E. Mercer, New York. A'Lelia Walker. Silver gelatin print, 1925. Schomburg Center for Research in Black Culture, NYPL.

 Unidentified man

 Edwin Harleston

 Unidentified man

Photographer: Elise Forrest Harleston, Charleston, S.C. Silver gelatin print, ca. 1920s. Edwina Whitlock Collection, Charleston, S.C.

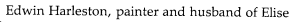
Edwin Harleston, painter and husband of Elise

Marie Forrest Harleston

Edwina Whitlock, age 5

Photographer: Walter Baker. Portrait of Cassie Dillard. Silver gelatin print, ca. 1920. Schomburg Center for Research in Black Culture, NYPL.

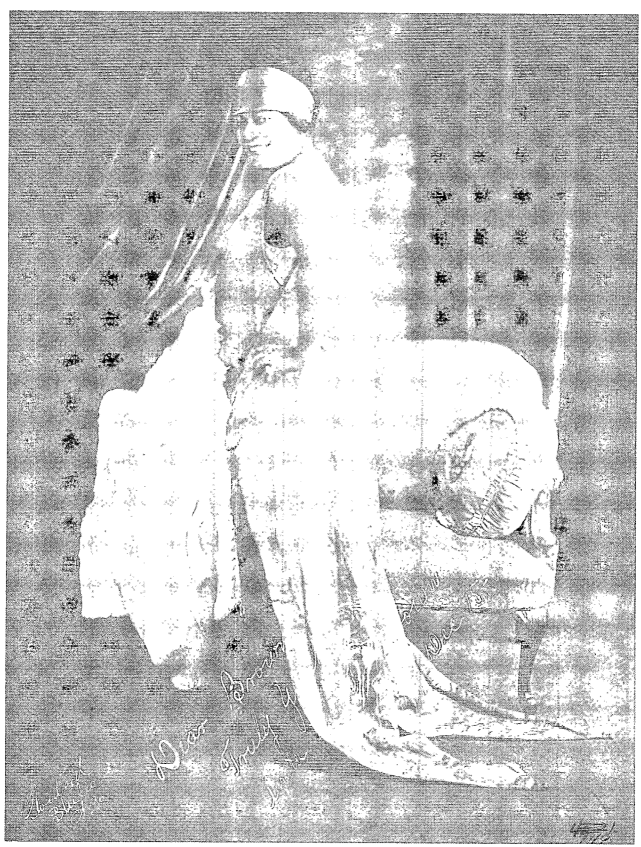

Photographer: Woodard Studio, Chicago. Anita Patti Brown. Gelatin silver print, 1923. Schomburg Center for Research in Black Culture, NYPL. Lawrence Brown Collection.

Photographer: E. Elcha, New York. Thelma Rhoten. Silver gelatin print, ca. 1920. Schomburg Center for Research in Black Culture, NYPL. Cutie Perkins Collection.

Photographer: E. Elcha. Unidentified portrait of a woman. Silver gelatin print, ca. 1920. Schomburg Center for Research in Black Culture, NYPL.

Photographer: E. Elcha, New York. Lafayette Theatre. Silver gelatin print, ca. 1920. Schomburg Center for Research in Black Culture, NYPL.

Photographer: E. Elcha, New York. Portrait of women basketball players. Silver gelatin print, 1924. Schomburg Center for Research in Black Culture, NYPL. Interstate Tattler Collection.

Photographer: E. Elcha, New York. Wilhemina Adams. Silver gelatin print, ca. 1930. Schomburg Center for Research in Black Culture, NYPL. Wilhemina Adams Collection.

Photographer: E. Elcha. The Musical Spillers. Silver gelatin print, 1922. Schomburg Center for Research in Black Culture, NYPL. Spiller Collection.

Photographer: Poole Studio, Atlanta. Panorama photograph of fraternity Alpha Phi Alpha. Silver gelatin print, 1929. Schomburg Center for Research in Black Culture, NYPL.

Photographer: Richard Roberts, Columbia, SC. Unidentified portrait of two children. Silver gelatin print (printed from a glass plate negative), ca. 1920s. Schomburg Center for Research in Black Culture, NYPL. Wilhemina Wynn Collection, New York.

Photographer: Richard Roberts, Columbia, SC. Unidentified family portrait. Silver gelatin print (printed from a glass plate negative), ca. 1930. Schomburg Center for Research in Black Culture, NYPL. Wilhemina Wynn Collection.

Photographer: Richard Roberts. Portrait of three women. Silver gelatin print (printed from a glass plate negative), ca. 1930. Schomburg Center for Research in Black Culture, NYPL. Wilhemina Wynn Collection, New York.

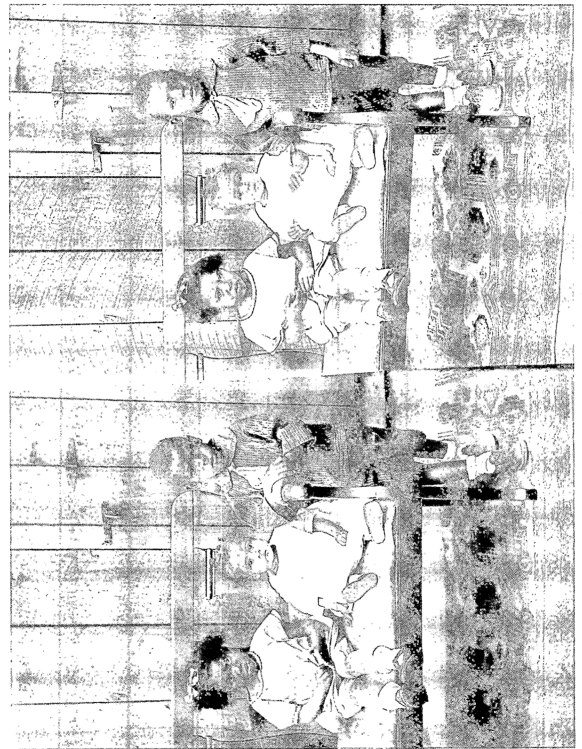

Photographer: Richard Roberts. Three children. Silver gelatin print (printed from a glass plate negative), ca. 1930. Schomburg Center for Research in Black Culture, NYPL. Wilhemina Wynn Collection, New York.

Robert McNeill, honor graduate of the New York Institute of Photography, and ace cameraman (Sadgwar Photo).

Photographer: Robert McNeill. William Hastie. Silver gelatin print, ca. 1930. Schomburg Center for Research in Black Culture, NYPL.

Photographer: Robert McNeill. Harold L. Ickes and Marian Anderson. Silver gelatin print, 1939. Schomburg Center for Research in Black Culture, NYPL.

Photographer: Edgar Phipps. Ralph Cooper. Silver gelatin print, ca. 1930. Schomburg Center for Research in Black Culture, NYPL.

Photographer: Edgar Phipps. Chorus Line. Silver gelatin print, ca. 1920s. Schomburg Center for Research in Black Culture, NYPL.

Photographer: Edgar Phipps, New York. Portrait of Lorraine (?). Silver gelatin print, 1943. Schomburg Center for Research in Black Culture, NYPL. Blanche Thomas Collection.

Photographer: James Latimer Allen. Arthur A. Schomburg. Silver gelatin print, ca. 1920s. Schomburg Center for Research in Black Culture, NYPL.

Photographer: James Latimer Allen. Countee Cullen. Silver gelatin print, ca 1930s. Schomburg Center for Research in Black Culture, NYPL.

Photographer: James Latimer Allen. Josephine Harreld Love. Silver gelatin print, ca. 1930s. Schomburg Center for Research in Black Culture, NYPL.

Photographer: James Latimer Allen. Alain Locke. Silver gelatin print, 1929. Schomburg Center for Research in Black Culture, NYPL.

Photographer: James Latimer Allen. Langston Hughes. Silver gelatin print, ca. 1920. Schomburg Center for Research in Black Culture, NYPL.

Photographer: James Latimer Allen. "Madonna and Child." Silver gelatin print, ca. 1930. Schomburg Center for Research in Black Culture, NYPL.

Photographer: James Latimer Allen. Claude McKay. Silver gelatin print, ca. 1930s. Schomburg Center for Research in Black Culture, NYPL.

Photographer: James Latimer Allen. Philippa Schuyler. Silver gelatin print, ca. 1940. Schomburg Center for Research in Black Culture, NYPL. Philippa Schuyler Collection.

Photographers: Morgan and Marvin Smith. Rev. Adam Clayton Powell, Sr. Silver gelatin print, 1938. Schomburg Center for Research in Black Culture, NYPL.

Photographers: Morgan and Marvin Smith. Rev. Adam Clayton Powell, Jr.
Silver gelatin print, 1938. Schomburg Center for Research in Black Culture,
NYPL.

Photographers: Morgan and Marvin Smith. Lindy Hoppers: Frank Manning and Ann Johnson. Silver gelatin print, 1941. Schomburg Center for Research in Black Culture, NYPL.

Photographers: Morgan and Marvin Smith. Pearl Bailey. Silver gelatin print, 1944. Schomburg Center for Research in Black Culture, NYPL.

Photographers: Morgan and Marvin Smith. Street Scene—Harlem. Silver gelatin print, 1938. Schomburg Center for Research in Black Culture, NYPL.

Photographer: Frank Cloud. Self-portrait. Silver gelatin print, ca. 1940. Doris Cloud Collection (Mrs. Frank), Los Angeles.

Photographer: Frank Cloud. Portrait of a Woman. Silver gelatin print, ca. 1940s. Doris Cloud Collection (Mrs. Frank), Los Angeles.

Photographer: Frank Cloud. Members of the Pacific Town Club of Los Angeles on a fishing trip. Silver gelatin print, ca. 1940s. Collection: Mrs. Doris Cloud (Mrs. Frank), Los Angeles.

Photographer: Gordon Parks. Richard Wright. Office of War Information. Silver gelatin print, ca. 1940s. Schomburg Center for Research in Black Culture, NYPL.

Photographer: Gordon Parks. Marian Anderson. Office of War Information. Silver gelatin print, ca. 1940. Schomburg Center for Research in Black Culture, NYPL.

Photographer: Gordon Parks. Miss Louise Washington. Farm Security Administration. Silver gelatin print, ca. 1939. Schomburg Center for Research in Black Culture, NYPL.

Photographer: Gordon Parks. Woman Cleaning Office. Office of War Information. Silver gelatin print, ca. 1940. Schomburg Center for Research in Black Culture, NYPL.

Photographer: P.H. Polk. Portrait of Alan Moton (?). Silver gelatin print, ca. 1940s. Schomburg Center for Research in Black Culture, NYPL.

Photographer: P.H. Polk. George Washington Carver. Silver gelatin print, 1943. Schomburg Center for Research in Black Culture, NYPL.

Photographer: Roy DeCarava. Two boys in vacant lot, NY. Silver gelatin print, 1949. Collection of photographer.

Photographer: Roy DeCarava. 117th Street, NY. Silver gelatin print, 1951. Collection of the photographer.

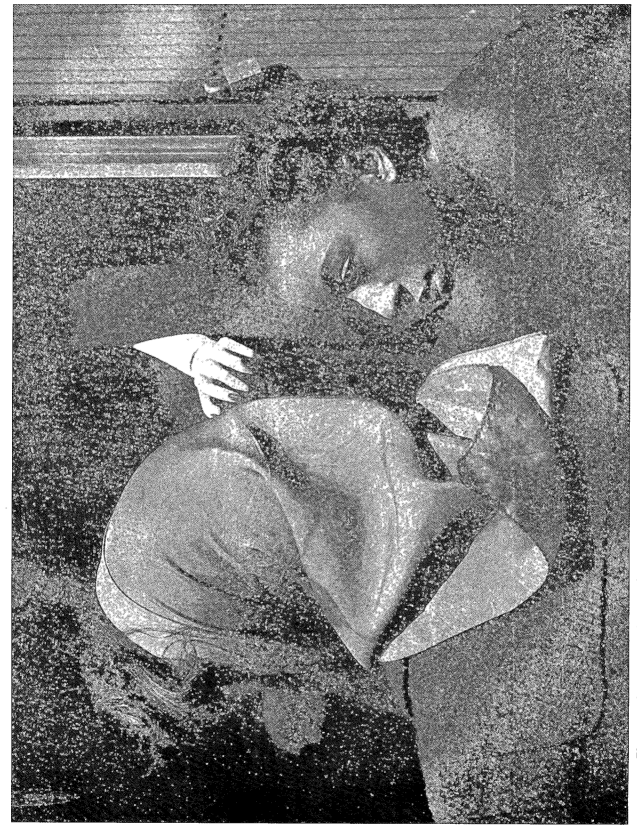

Photographer: Roy DeCarava.   Two women and mannequin's hand.   Silver gelatin print, 1950. Collection of photographer.

Photographer: Austin Hansen. Street Scene—Harlem. Silver gelatin print, ca. 1950s. Schomburg Center for Research in Black Culture, NYPL.

Photographer: Austin Hansen. Pulpit of the St. Luke AME Church, New York. Silver gelatin print, ca. 1950s. Schomburg Center for Research in Black Culture, NYPL.

Photographer: Austin Hansen. Confirmation Class, St. Martin's Church, New York. Silver gelatin print, 1967. Schomburg Center for Research in Black Culture, NYPL.

Photographer: Austin Hansen. Percy Sutton. Silver gelatin print, ca. 1960s. Schomburg Center for Research in Black Culture, NYPL.

Cites areas where these artists were/are active.

ALABAMA

Tuskegee
  Battey, Cornelius M.
  Bedou, Arthur P.
  Polk, P.H.

ARKANSAS

Little Rock
  Bryant, Hayward

CALIFORNIA

Los Angeles
  Cloud, Frank Herman
  Smith, Frank G.
  Spigner, W.H.S.
Sacramento
  Ross, W.H.
San Francisco
  Grice, Francis
  Myzell, Thestus

CONNECTICUT

Hartford
  Asher, Eldridge
  Washington, Augustus

DISTRICT OF COLUMBIA

  Freeman, Daniel
  Keith, DeWitt
  McNeill, Robert
  Scurlock, Addison N.

FLORIDA

Jacksonville
  Weems, Ellis L.

GEORGIA

  Poole, Paul

ILLINOIS

Chicago
  Ganaway, King Daniel
  Lee, Edward Henry
  Perryman, F.R.
  Webb, Miles
  Woodward Studios

KANSAS

Kansas City
  Minter, G.W.

KENTUCKY

Louisville
  Husband, Harvey
  Lawson, W.H.

LOUISIANA

New Orleans
  Bedou, Arthur P.
  Lion, Jules

MARYLAND

Baltimore
  Macbeth, Arthur

MASSACHUSETTS

Boston
  Bailey, John B.
  Bannister, Edward
    Mitchell
  Collins, Herbert
  Smith, Hamilton

MICHIGAN

Saginaw
  Goodridge Brothers
  Gray, J.H.

MINNESOTA

Minneapolis
  Ball, James Presley
St. Paul
  Beasley, D.E.
  Shepherd, Harry (Henry)

MISSISSIPPI

Natchez
  Lynch, John Roy

MISSOURI

Mexico
  Miller, J.W.

MONTANA

Helena
  Ball, James Presley

NEW YORK

New York City
  Allen, James Latimer
  Battey, Cornelius M.
  Boyd, Walter A.
  Campbell, James S.
  DeCarava, Roy
  Elcha, Eddie
  Hansen, Austin
  Higgins, Benjamin L.
  Mercer, R.E.
  Parks, Gordon
  Phipps, Edgar
  Smith, Morgan and Marvin
  Van Der Zee, James
Syracuse
  Barnes, J.F.
  Stephens, Walter J.

OHIO

Cincinnati
  Ball, James Presley
  Ball, Thomas
  Duncanson, Robert Scott
Cleveland
  Baker, Hattie
Dayton
  Jackson, Andrew F.
Springfield
  Bowdre, Hayes Louis
  Hunster, Lewis P.
Toledo
  Fields, George

PENNSYLVANIA

Philadelphia
  Davis, C.J.
Wilkes-Barre
  Johnson, John W.
York
  Goodridge Brothers
  Gray, J.H.

SOUTH CAROLINA

Charleston
  Harleston, Elise Forrest
Columbia
  Roberts, Richard S.

TENNESSEE

   Knoxville
     Browder, B.B.
   Memphis
     Taylor, L.O.
     Thompson, Fannie J.

VIRGINIA

   Norfolk
     Macbeth, Arthur
   Richmond
     Farley, James Conway

WASHINGTON

   Seattle
     Ball, James Presley

PUBLIC

African Meeting House,
Boston, Massachusetts

Amistad Research Center,
New Orleans, Louisiana

Center for Southern Folklore,
Memphis, Tennessee

Central Michigan University, Clark Historical Library,
Mt. Pleasant, Michigan

Cincinnati Public Library,
Cincinnati, Ohio

Connecticut Historical Society,
Hartford, Connecticut

Corcoran Gallery of Art,
Washington, D.C.

Harmon Foundation, National Archives and Records Service,
Washington, D.C.

The Historic New Orleans Collection,
New Orleans, Louisiana

Howard University, Moorland Spingarn Research Center,
Washington, D.C.

Hoyt Library,
Saginaw, Michigan

Library of Congress,
Washington, D.C.

Library of Congress, Farm Security Administration,
Washington, D.C.

Metropolitan Museum of Art,
New York, New York

Minnesota Historical Society,
St. Paul, Minnesota

Montana Historical Society,
Helena, Montana

New York Public Library, Prints and Photographs Division,
New York, New York

New York Public Library, Schomburg Center for Research
   in Black Culture,
New York, New York

Saginaw County Historical Society Museum,
Saginaw, Michigan

Saginaw News
Saginaw, Michigan

Studio Museum in Harlem,
New York, New York

Tuskegee Institute,
Tuskegee, Alabama

U.S. Army Signal Corps, National Archives and Records
   Service,
Washington, D.C.

Valentine Museum,
Richmond, Virginia

Virginia Historical Society,
Richmond, Virginia

Yale University,
James Weldon Johnson Memorial Collection of Negro Arts
   and Letters,
New Haven, Connecticut

PRIVATE

de Abajian, James T.,
San Francisco, California

Barboza, Anthony,
New York, New York

Bundles, A'Leila,
Atlanta, Georgia

Cloud, Frank H. (Mrs. Doris),
Los Angeles, California

Gross, Larry,
New York, New York

Hansen, Austin,
New York, New York

Jezierski, John,
Saginaw, Michigan

Keith, DeWitt (Mrs. Doris),
Washington, D.C.

Lawrence, Betty,
Philadelphia, Pennsylvania

Lunn Gallery,
Washington, D.C.

Nelson, Stanley,
New York, New York

Nexus Gallery,
Atlanta, Georgia

Parks, Gordon,
New York, New York

Polk, P.H.,
Tuskegee, D.C.

Scurlock Studios,
Washington, D.C.

Smith, Morgan and Marvin,
New York, New York

Van Der Zee, James (Mrs. Donna Mussenden),
New York, New York

Weems, Ellis,
Jacksonville, Florida

Whitlock, Edwina Harleston,
Charleston, South Carolina

Wynn, Wilhemina,
New York, New York